Nourish your Soul

stewed!®

80 IRRESISTIBLE STEWS AND ONE-POT WONDERS

stewed!

NOURISH YOUR SOUL

80 IRRESISTIBLE STEWS AND ONE-POT WONDERS

Alan Rosenthal

EBURY
PRESS

10 9 8 7 6 5 4 3 2

Published in 2010 by Ebury Press, an imprint of Ebury Publishing
Ebury Publishing is a division of the Random House Group

Text © Alan Rosenthal 2010
Photography by Jonathan Gregson

The Random House Group Limited Reg. No. 954009

Addresses for companies within the Random House Group can be found at www.randomhouse.co.uk

A CIP catalogue record for this book is available from the British Library

The Random House Group Limited supports The Forest Stewardship Council (FSC), the leading international forest certification organisation. All our titles that are printed on Greenpeace approved FSC certified paper carry the FSC logo. Our paper procurement policy can be found at www.randomhouse.co.uk/environment

Design: Inga Wilmink
Photographer: Jonathan Gregson
Copy editor: Helena Caldon

Many thanks to istockphoto and dreamstime for the use of additional images in this book.

Printed in Italy by Graphicom srl

ISBN: 9780091938024

To buy books by your favourite authors and register for offers visit www.randomhouse.co.uk

CONTENTS

INTRODUCTION

It was an incredible feeling when, on 6 April 2008, I sold my first pot of stew at the Alexandra Palace farmers' market in north London.

However, the day didn't exactly begin according to plan. I woke up, in horror, to a pristine layer of snow, 2 or 3 inches thick, lying on the ground. I love snow normally but this was not the day for it. 'How am I going to get to the market in all this snow?' I thought, 'How are my helpers going to get there?' More importantly, were there going to be any punters venturing out into the cold and snowy day to buy my wares? I'd spent weeks preparing for this moment and had been cooking for days. Snow was not a part of the plan and panic set in!

In the end, everything turned out just fine and I now see snow as a good omen; indeed, just under two years after the first pot was sold, the white stuff made an appearance once again for the national launch of **stewed!** in one of the UK's largest supermarket chains.

The **stewed!** journey has been an exciting one for me, fuelled with many challenges, twists and turns that I wasn't expecting at the start. I've learnt more than at any other time in my career, and often I'm amazed at what's actually happened over the last two years.

My career path before **stewed!** was a little convoluted. I'd always loved food and cooking but I'd never really been down that path professionally, so finally, after becoming disillusioned at work in 2007, I decided to quit and follow my heart. I spent three months brushing up on my cooking skills before working as a private chef on a vineyard near Bordeaux, in France. I then returned to London and tried my hand in restaurant kitchens for a few months – quite an experience!

However, something just didn't feel right and every day a little voice kept reminding me of an idea I had a year or so beforehand whilst sitting on a circle line train on the London underground. The idea was stew; I was convinced there was a gap in the market. So in January 2008, I finally listened to the little voice and took the plunge and **stewed!** was born.

Two years on, people often ask me, 'How did you do it?' The reality is simply that I had an idea I believed in and went for it, followed my instincts, found the best people to help me on my journey and made it happen. So my advice would be, if you've got an idea that you believe in, go for it!

WHY STEWS AND ONE-POT WONDERS?

I always find there's something incredibly satisfying about preparing and eating a stew; a medley of raw ingredients cooked together in a single pot to create a delicious symphony of flavours and textures. They also add theatre to mealtimes; a great big steaming cauldron taking centre stage for people to dig in to. We're talking communal food that works just as well for dinner parties as it does for casual lunches. More importantly, because most can be made ahead of schedule, you, the cook, can sit back and enjoy the occasion rather than worrying about a complicated dish that needs your undivided attention at the last minute.

In the UK, we associate stews and one-pot dishes with winter; food to warm us up on a cold day. But in reality, these kinds of dishes exist all over the world, in hot climates as well as cold; slow-cooked curries from India, beef rendang from Malaysia, aromatic lamb tagine from Morocco, as well as European classics like boeuf Bourguignon, Irish stew, paella... the list is endless.

The recipes in this book are designed to give you a flavour of a range of stews and one-pot dishes from around the world – and there's quite a mix. Although the majority are pretty simple to make, there are a few things to be aware of and I've summarised them below.

Cooking pots

Always use heavy based saucepans and flameproof casserole dishes for the recipes in this book. Several require a lid, so be sure to check this before you start.

Choosing your meat

The joy of stews and one-pot dishes is that you can often get away with using cheaper cuts of meat, as the slow cooking will tenderise them beautifully and bring out their flavour. That being said, those cheaper cuts of chicken and beef can cause some confusion, so here's a little advice:

Chicken

I suggest using chicken thighs in the majority of recipes in this book. Thigh meat stays much more moist during long, slow cooking so is perfect for stews and casseroles. To be honest, though, I think thighs taste so much better than breast anyway, even when only cooked for a short time. Breast is definitely not best in my book!

Beef

Avoid braising steak and go for chuck steak instead. Braising steak tends to be quite a dense grain, which gives the meat a dry and grainy texture. Chuck steak, however, has more of an open structure thanks to its fat and connective tissue. Once it's trimmed of any excess fat and cooked for a couple of hours, it'll be meltingly tender and soft with none of the graininess of braising steak.

Stocks

Several of the recipes in this book call for stock. After much deliberation, though, I decided not to include any separate stock recipes. These days you can easily buy decent fresh stocks in the supermarket. Although they won't be as good as home-made, I think they're fine to use.

However, do check the salt content as it's better to use salt-free varieties if at all possible. If your only option is to use a powder or stock cube, don't add any salt to the recipe until you've tasted the cooked dish. You can always add more salt but you can't take it away!

Browning meat

Browning meat is a crucial part in the cooking of many stews, especially those from Europe or the New World. It'll give your stew both good colour and flavour, so it's important that it's done properly.

Firstly, the oil or butter in your pan should be hot before adding the meat so that it seals it the moment it touches the pan. This prevents juices from escaping and the build-up of steam which stops the meat from browning.

The next thing to keep in mind is not to crowd the pan, so brown meat in batches, adding a little more oil if you need to after each batch. You need about 1cm of free space around each piece of meat in the pan to avoid steam building up. This also prevents the pan from cooling too quickly. Don't be tempted to move the pieces of meat too frequently; instead allow them to cook for a couple of minutes or so first. This will encourage good colour and again prevent juices from escaping. It's also important to get the right level of heat. Too hot and the pan will burn, too low and your meat will steam.

A burnt pan will flavour your entire stew if you were to carry on using it. If you do burn the base of your pan, simply wash it out thoroughly, add fresh oil and continue where you left off. If the pan looks quite dark but not actually burnt (smell it − you can tell if it's burnt!), rinse it with a little water, reserve the water and use this to make up the liquid content in the recipe, it'll add good flavour. Then dry the pan, add fresh oil and carry on.

If you follow these guidelines you should achieve nicely browned meat.

Nourish your Soul

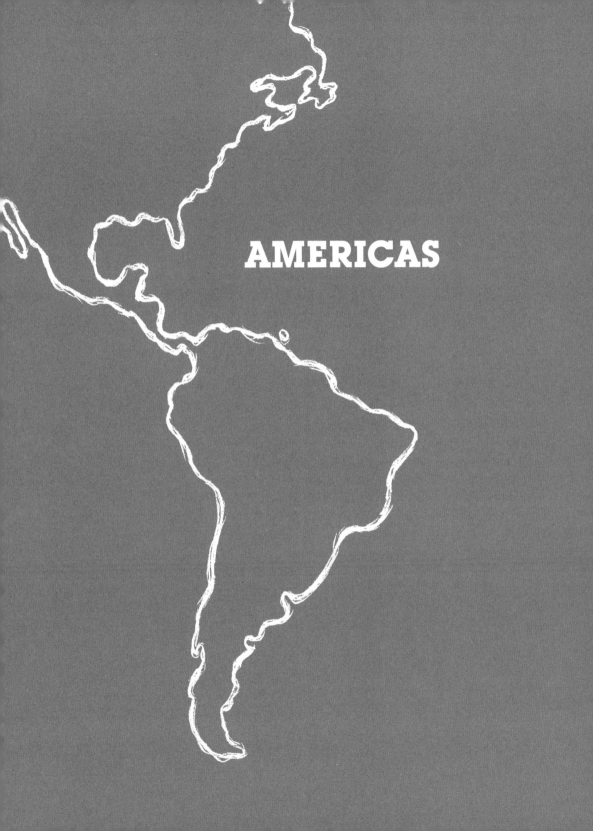

AMERICAS

BOSTON BAKED BEANS

We all grew up on baked beans, but this is the real thing! I cooked this recipe for one of the 'stew parties' I threw to help me choose which recipes to include in the book. My intrepid tasters described it as 'baked beans for adults' and just like 'cowboy food'. Take their word for it – it's superb.

Serves 4–6

400g dried haricot beans
3 onions, quartered
5 cloves
60g muscovado sugar
50g black treacle
50g ketchup
1 tbsp English mustard (made from powder)
2 tbsp red wine vinegar
800g pork belly, rind removed and cut into 3–4cm cubes
salt and freshly ground black pepper

Soak the haricot beans overnight, covered with at least 8cm of water.

The next day, preheat the oven to 160°C/325°F/Fan 150°C/gas mark 3. Rinse the soaked beans and put them in a heavy based, ovenproof pan that has a lid. Cover with 5cm of water, bring to simmering point and cook for about 40 minutes until nearly tender. Top up with a little boiling water if it looks too dry (you want the beans to be covered at all times).

Stud the onion quarters with the cloves and add these to the pot with the sugar, treacle, ketchup, mustard, vinegar, pork and some grinds of the pepper mill (don't add salt at this stage as it can toughen the beans). Pop the pan, with the lid on, into the oven for 2½–3 hours until the beans are creamy and soft and the pork completely tender. You may need to remove the lid for the final 30 minutes to drive off most of the remaining liquid. Give it a taste for saltiness, and season according to your taste buds.

Serve with nothing more than some crusty bread and a salad.

CHICKEN AND PRAWN JAMBALAYA

Clearly a cousin of Spanish paella, jambalaya (page 17) also has the hallmarks of French and Caribbean cuisine. There aren't any hard-and-fast rules as to how to make a jambalaya; this version, also known as Creole jambalaya, uses tomatoes to give colour and flavour to the rice. A variety of meats can be used as this dish was traditionally poor man's food, made with pretty much any meat you could find – from alligator to turtle. This recipe makes life easy using chicken thighs, prawns and chorizo sausage.

Serves 4–6

2 tbsp olive oil
150g chorizo, sliced
4 chicken thighs (about 500g in total), skin on
3 bay leaves
1 onion, finely chopped
1 large red pepper, cut into quarters lengthways
then sliced into 5mm strips
1 celery stick, finely chopped
1 long hot red chilli, deseeded and thinly sliced
3 garlic cloves, finely chopped
2 sprigs of thyme
2 pinches of ground cloves
250g tinned chopped tomatoes
700ml chicken stock
150g prawns, shell on but heads removed and reserved
salt and freshly ground black pepper
300g long grain rice or basmati
3 spring onions, finely chopped
4 tbsp chopped fresh parsley
juice of ½ lemon

To serve:
lemon wedges
chopped fresh parsley

Heat the oil in a large, fairly deep pan that has a lid. Add the chorizo slices and cook for a couple of minutes until the chorizo lets out its paprika oils and starts to brown a little. Remove with a slotted spoon and reserve for later.

Season the chicken thighs and add to the hot oil, skin-side down, along with the bay leaves and cook for 5–7 minutes on a moderate heat until golden brown. Then turn over the thighs and cook them on the other side for a minute to seal before removing and setting aside on a plate.

Add the onion, red pepper, celery, chilli, garlic and thyme to the pan and cook gently for 10 minutes until the peppers and onions have softened. Add the ground cloves and cook for another couple of minutes, then mix in the tomatoes and cook for a further 5 minutes until the tomatoes have turned pulpy.

Add the chicken stock, the reserved prawn heads and a few pinches of salt and grinds of black pepper. Give it all a good stir and bring to simmering point. Now return the chorizo (and any oils that have tried to escape) as well as the chicken (and any juices that have collected) to the pan. Cover with a lid and simmer gently for 25 minutes to cook the chicken through.

Remove the prawn heads and add the rice to the pan, stirring it around to distribute it evenly. Cover again with the lid and cook for 20 minutes. Give it a stir every 5 minutes or so. If it's looking at all dry, add a little water – the jambalaya is meant to be quite moist.

Once the 20 minutes is up, mix in the raw prawns, replace the lid and cook for a further 5 minutes.

Finally, stir through the chopped spring onions and parsley and squeeze over the lemon juice. Serve in a deep bowl with lemon wedges and some more parsley scattered over.

FEIJOADA – BRAZILIAN BLACK BEAN STEW
with chorizo and smoked pork

Feijoada (page 16) is a national dish of Brazil. When I was on the markets selling stews, a Brazilian lady sold pies next to me. She always said I should try making *feijoada* and I'm pleased I did! A variety of meats are often used but here things are kept simple with some smoked gammon, cooking chorizo and pork shoulder. Few other ingredients give a stew such a colour as black beans, but don't be put off – it'll taste delicious!

Serves 4–6

400g dried black beans
2 bay leaves
200g cooking chorizo sausages,
cut into large chunks
200g pork shoulder,
cut into 3–4cm pieces
350g smoked gammon
(rind removed), cut into 3–4cm pieces
salt and freshly ground black pepper

2 tbsp olive oil
100g smoked lardons
2 onions, roughly chopped
3 garlic cloves, roughly chopped

To serve:
2 oranges, sliced
2 tbsp chopped fresh coriander

Soak the black beans overnight, covered with at least 8cm of water.

The next day, rinse and drain the soaked beans and put them in a large heavy based pan. Cover with 5cm of water, add the bay leaves, bring to simmering point and cook for 1¼ hours. Add the chorizo, pork and smoked gammon to the pan along with a few grinds of the pepper mill, then continue to cook on the hob, uncovered, on a low heat for a further 1½ hours, by which time the beans should have softened.

Heat the oil in a frying pan, brown the lardons and then add the onions. Cook gently for 10–12 minutes until the onions are starting to colour, then add the chopped garlic for another couple of minutes. Once nicely coloured, take a few spoonfuls of the softened black beans and mash them into the onion mixture. Tip the mixture into the pot with the rest of the cooking pork and black beans (this will help the liquor to thicken) and continue cooking for a further 30–40 minutes until the beans are starting to break down and the meat is completely tender. Taste for seasoning as you may not need any salt depending on how salty your chorizo is.

Serve accompanied by slices of orange and some chopped coriander.

NEW ENGLAND CLAM CHOWDER

There seem to be two schools of thought when it comes to clam chowder; you either go for the 'tomatoey' version from Manhattan or the creamy version from New England. I've gone for the creamy version as recommended by Sandy, the American mother of a friend who made this for me once when I stayed at their house.

Serves 4

30g butter
60g streaky bacon,
cut into 5mm strips
1 onion, finely sliced
1 leek, finely sliced
1 bay leaf
2 tbsp plain flour
600g medium floury potatoes
(about 4 medium potatoes), peeled
and cut into 1cm pieces

500ml milk
1kg clams, scrubbed and cleaned
salt and freshly ground black pepper
3 tbsp double cream
a handful of finely chopped chives

Melt the butter in a heavy pan, then gently brown the bacon for about 5 minutes, taking care not to burn the butter. Add the onion and leek as well as the bay leaf and cook gently with the lid on the pan for about 15 minutes until the onions and leeks are very soft.

Add the flour and stir well. Continue cooking for a couple of minutes before adding the potatoes and then the milk to the pan – the milk should cover the potatoes. Bring back to simmering point and cook gently for 15–20 minutes or until the potatoes are tender. Make sure you stir the pan regularly, otherwise things have a tendency to stick.

Meanwhile, put the clams in a separate deep pan with a splash of water. Cover the pan with a lid and cook for 5–10 minutes until the clams have opened. Once cooked, allow them to cool a little before removing the meat from the shells. Discard any shells that have not opened. Strain the liquor through a sieve lined with kitchen paper (to remove all the grit) and set aside.

Once the potatoes are cooked, add the clam meat and the strained clam liquor to them and bring back to simmering point. Taste before adding salt (if needed) and black pepper. Finish the chowder by stirring through the cream and chopped chives.

SECO DE CORDERO – PERUVIAN LAMB STEW
with coriander and beer

Serves 4

3 tbsp olive oil
900g lamb shoulder, excess fat removed
and cut into 3–4cm cubes
salt and freshly ground black pepper
2 red onions, finely sliced
8 garlic cloves, finely chopped
1 hot fresh chilli, finely sliced
(include seeds)
1½ tsp ground cumin

400ml beer
3 tbsp red wine vinegar
1 large bunch coriander (about 140g),
stems removed and tied with a piece
of string
2 tomatoes, roughly chopped
400g potatoes, peeled and chopped into
2cm cubes

Heat the oil in a casserole dish that has a lid, season the lamb with salt and black pepper and brown the pieces in the hot oil, in batches, for about 5 minutes. Set aside the browned meat in a bowl.

Throw the onions into the pan, adding a little more oil and a splash of water if it feels too dry. Cook gently for about 10 minutes until the onions have softened. Then add the garlic, chilli and cumin and continue to cook for another couple of minutes.

Add the beer, vinegar, the tied coriander stalks, tomatoes and some salt and black pepper to the pan. Give it all a good stir and finally add the browned lamb and any juices to the pan. Cook gently for 1¼ hours with the lid of the pan set on a slight slant to let some steam escape.

After 1¼ hours, remove the coriander stalks from the pan and add the potatoes, pushing the pieces into the stew. Continue cooking gently for a further 30 minutes or until the potatoes are cooked. You're after a fairly thick sauce, so if it's looking a little liquid, finish the cooking with the lid off.

Once the potatoes are cooked and the lamb is tender, finely chop the leaves from the coriander and stir them through the stew. Check for seasoning, adding some more salt and black pepper if it needs it.

CHILLI CON CARNE

You can't buy a good chilli in the shops, so I say make it yourself. Thanks go to my friend Sally who suggested the addition of some honey or maple syrup to the recipe. I also like to use small chunks of beef rather than mince, but feel free to use mince if you want to.

Serves 6

2 tbsp olive oil
2 onions, roughly chopped
3 garlic cloves, roughly chopped
pinch of cinnamon
½–1 tsp cayenne pepper (you can
add less if you don't want it so hot)
1 tsp dried oregano
1 tsp ground cumin
800g beef chuck steak,
cut into 1cm pieces
400g tin chopped tomatoes
60g tomato purée
2 tbsp maple syrup or honey

1 red pepper, roughly chopped
1 green pepper, roughly chopped
150ml red wine
salt and freshly ground black pepper
240g tin kidney beans,
rinsed and drained
20g plain chocolate
(at least 70% cocoa solids – I used Divine)

To serve:
fresh lime juice
chopped fresh coriander
grated Cheddar

Heat the oil in a heavy based, flameproof casserole dish and soften the onions. When the onions are soft and translucent, after about 10 minutes, add the garlic, cinnamon, cayenne pepper, oregano and cumin to the pan. Cook for a couple of minutes before adding the chunks of beef.

After about 5 minutes, once the beef has browned on all sides, add the tomatoes, tomato purée, maple syrup (or honey), red and green peppers and wine. Mix everything well, add some salt and black pepper, then bring the mixture to simmering point and cook, covered, on the hob for 1½ hours. If it's getting too dry at any time, add a little water.

When the time is up, add the kidney beans and continue cooking for a further 30 minutes, but this time keep the pot uncovered.

Once the chilli is cooked and has thickened, stir in the chocolate and taste for seasoning.

Serve with a squeeze of fresh lime, some chopped coriander and grated Cheddar alongside some fluffy rice. (Offer some sour cream and guacamole, too, if you like.)

BAHIAN CHICKEN STEW

This recipe comes from my friend Christie's mum (Christie was chief stew-potter in the early days of **stewed!**). It's a real family heirloom that has been handed down through a couple of generations. I have to confess, I'd never heard of this stew until Christie submitted it as potential for the **stewed!** cook book. This is one of those life-saver recipes when you have to rustle something up pretty quick.

Serves 4–6

juice of 3 limes
salt and freshly ground black pepper
8 chicken thighs (about 1kg in total), skin on
1 tbsp olive oil
1 onion, roughly chopped
1 red pepper, roughly chopped
4 garlic cloves, finely chopped
1 long mild red chilli, deseeded and finely sliced
2 tomatoes, roughly chopped or ½ tin chopped tomatoes
150ml coconut milk
50g skinless peanuts, finely chopped*
100g shelled raw prawns (optional)

To serve:
some lime wedges and chopped fresh coriander

Mix half the lime juice with a few pinches of salt in a bowl. Add the chicken and rub the marinade over the thighs. Cover and leave for 30 minutes to an hour.

Heat the oil in a deep, non-stick frying pan or in a flameproof casserole dish. Shake off any excess marinade and fry the chicken, skin-side down, for 5–7 minutes or until golden brown (do this in batches if you need to). Turn them over and seal the other side for about a minute. Set aside the browned pieces on a plate.

Fry the onion and red pepper in the same pan for 10–12 minutes until soft and the onions are starting to turn brown, then add the garlic and chilli and cook for a couple of minutes, stirring occasionally before adding the tomatoes. Cook for another 10 minutes before finally adding the coconut milk, peanuts, black pepper and a couple of good pinches of salt to the pan. Give everything a good stir and then plop the pieces of chicken back in, skin-side up, along with any juices that may have collected.

Cook on a medium heat for 30–40 minutes until the chicken has cooked and the sauce reduced. If you decide to make the dish with the addition of prawns, add them about 5 minutes before the end of the cooking time.

When the chicken is cooked, mix in the remaining lime juice and taste for seasoning. Serve with lime wedges and a sprinkling of chopped coriander alongside some steamed rice.

* I found it impossible to buy skinless raw peanuts. If you, like me, have this problem, buy ones with skins on, bake them in the oven at 190°C/375°F/Fan 180°C/gas mark 5 for about 5 minutes until they start popping. Once the peanuts have cooled a little you'll be able to remove the skins by rubbing them vigorously in a tea towel. Hopefully you can save yourself the hassle by finding some in the shops!

Tip – The chicken can be replaced with chunks of white fish. Marinate the fish in the same way as the chicken, then follow the instructions above from the onion cooking onwards. After the sauce part of the stew has been cooking gently for about 20 minutes, add your fish and prawns, if using.

TOMATICAN
Pork stewed in tomatoes, oregano and cumin with fresh sweetcorn

My Argentinean friend, Andrea, introduced me to this stew. It's a really good one for summer as it's quite light and great served at room temperature as well as direct from the hob.

Serves 6

4 tbsp olive oil
1kg pork shoulder, cut into 3–4cm pieces
2 onions, thinly sliced
3 garlic cloves, roughly chopped
3 tsp dried oregano
(more if using it fresh)
2 tsp ground cumin
900g cherry tomatoes, halved
salt and freshly ground black pepper

3 corn cobs – 2 with the kernels
sliced off, 1 cut into 6 pieces
sugar (if needed)

To serve:
chopped fresh coriander
1 red chilli, thinly sliced

Heat the oil in a wide saucepan that has a lid, then brown the pork in batches and set aside in a bowl.

Add the onions to the pan with a splash of water and some more oil if it's looking too dry. Cook gently for 10–15 minutes until very soft and starting to brown at the edges. Add the garlic, oregano and cumin and cook for a couple of minutes, then throw in the tomatoes and let them break down on a moderate heat for 5–10 minutes before returning the pork and any juices to the pan. Stir through a good few pinches of salt and some grinds of black pepper. Cover with the lid and cook gently for 1–1½ hours until the pork is tender.

Once the meat is tender, stir in the corn kernels and the cob pieces and cook, without the lid, for another 5–10 minutes until the corn is done.

Taste for seasoning; if your tomatoes were quite acidic you may need to add a little sugar to balance this. Serve garnished with some chopped coriander and a few chilli slices.

SUCCOTASH
of sweetcorn, butternut squash and broad beans

Succotash is a traditional dish of native Americans that always consisted of sweetcorn kernels and usually broad beans. This adaptation adds some sweet butternut squash and soured cream to the recipe, creating a delicious, fresh, sweet vegetable stew that's great either hot or served at room temperature.

Serves 4

50g butter
1 red onion, finely sliced
1 red pepper, quartered, deseeded
and cut into 5mm slices
2 garlic cloves, finely chopped
300g peeled butternut squash,
diced into 1½cm pieces
(try to find top-quality, extra-sweet squash)

200ml vegetable stock
kernels from 3 corn cobs
200g fresh young broad beans (if you
can't find fresh, then frozen peas work
quite well, albeit rather smaller), cooked
3 spring onions, finely sliced
3–4 tbsp soured cream
salt and freshly ground black pepper

Melt the butter in a wide pan that has a lid. Add the onion and red pepper and cook gently for 10 minutes until the onion has softened. Then add the garlic and butternut squash. Cook for a couple of minutes.

Add the stock and cover the pan with a lid. Cook gently for about 3 minutes. Now add the corn kernels and cover again, continuing to cook for about 5 minutes until the corn is tender and the squash has cooked through. Stir through the broad beans (or peas) and two-thirds of the spring onions to warm through. Finish by stirring in the soured cream, adding salt and black pepper to taste and sprinkling with the remaining spring onions.

Perfect with some crusty bread.

BRITISH ISLES

MUSSELS WITH CIDER AND LEEKS

Replace onions with leeks and white wine with cider and you've got a British take on the classic moules marinières that comes from the other side of the Channel. Serve with big chunks of bread to mop up all the delicious juices.

It's best to buy mussels in the cooler months when they are in season, plump and juicy.

Serves 4

60g butter
1 large leek, cleaned, tough outer leaves removed and finely sliced
2 garlic cloves, finely chopped
2 bay leaves
freshly ground black pepper
3kg mussels, washed, scraped and beards removed
300ml English cider
6 tbsp roughly chopped parsley
6 tbsp double cream

Melt the butter in a very large, deep saucepan that has a lid, add the leek, garlic, bay leaves and a few good grinds of your pepper mill and cook very gently for about 15 minutes until the leeks are very soft but not caramelised.

Then simply throw in the mussels, pour in the cider and grind over some black pepper. Give everything a good stir, turn up the heat and cover the pan. Cook for about 5 minutes until the mussels have opened. Discard any shells that have not opened.

Throw over the parsley, pour in the double cream and give the mussels a good stir. That's it!

CHICKEN STEW
with cider, tarragon and asparagus

Tarragon chicken is a classic – this is the **stewed!** version.

Serves 4

100g smoked lardons
3 tbsp olive oil
25g butter
2 onions, roughly chopped
1 leek, cut into ½cm slices
2 garlic cloves, finely chopped
salt and freshly ground black pepper
8 chicken thighs (about 1kg), skin on
1 tbsp plain flour

500ml English cider
250ml chicken stock
2 tbsp grain mustard
2 carrots, peeled and cut into 2cm chunks
bunch of tarragon (left whole)
2 bay leaves
12 small asparagus spears
1 tbsp chopped tarragon
3 tbsp crème fraîche

In a large pan that has a lid, gently fry the lardons in 1 tablespoon of the oil until they've turned golden brown at the edges and the fat has melted away. Add the butter to the pan and once melted throw in the onions, leek and garlic. Cook very gently on a low heat for 10–15 minutes until the onions and leeks are soft and transparent.

Meanwhile, in a non-stick frying pan, heat the remaining oil. Season the chicken and gently fry the thighs in batches, skin-side down, for 5–7 minutes until the skin is a deep golden colour and crispy. Fry the other side for a couple of minutes. Transfer each browned batch to a plate.

When the onions and leeks have softened, add the flour, stir and cook for a couple of minutes before adding the cider, stock, mustard, carrots and a couple of good pinches of salt and some grinds of pepper. Then add the bunch of tarragon and the bay leaves, followed by the browned chicken thighs, skin-side up. Cover and cook gently on the hob for 40 minutes.

Remove the bunch of tarragon and continue to cook, with the lid off, for 1 hour. If you think the chicken is getting dry, add a little water.

Meanwhile, blanch some asparagus stalks by plunging them into a pan of boiling water for a couple of minutes, then rinsing them in cold water. Set aside.

The sauce should have thickened now and the chicken should be nice and tender. Turn off the heat and add the chopped tarragon and crème fraîche, stirring to combine. Taste for seasoning, adjusting if necessary with some extra salt and black pepper.

Stir in the asparagus to warm through and serve simply with a few boiled new potatoes.

CULLEN SKINK

I discovered Cullen skink (page 40, bottom) in Scotland when I was at university at St Andrews studying for my degree. Although traditionally more of a soup that originated from the small fishing village of Cullen, I think it also makes a great stew by simply adding less milk. I love smoked haddock and this is a really simple recipe in which you can enjoy it at its best.

Serves 4–6

60g butter
1 onion, finely sliced
1 leek, finely sliced
600g floury potatoes,
peeled and cut into 2–3cm chunks
600ml whole milk
1 bay leaf
freshly grated nutmeg

600g undyed smoked haddock,
skinned and cut into 5cm pieces
salt and freshly ground black pepper

To serve:
grated mature Cheddar
chopped fresh parsley

Melt 45g of the butter in a heavy based pan that has a lid. Add the onion and leek and gently sweat them, with the lid on the pan, for 15–20 minutes until they are extremely soft and almost sweet.

Next add the chunks of potato and cook gently, again with the lid on, for a further 10 minutes until the potatoes are starting to soften a little.

Add the milk, bay leaf and a little grated nutmeg. Bring up to simmering point, adding some black pepper to the pan. Cook gently for 20–25 minutes until the potatoes are very soft and beginning to break up, then turn off the heat and squash some of the potatoes with the back of a fork into the milk to thicken it. Stir in the smoked haddock pieces, cover with the lid, and leave for 5 minutes off the heat to allow the haddock to just cook.

Lift off the lid and stir gently to combine all the flavours, trying not break up the fish too much. Have a taste and depending on the cure of the haddock you may need to add some more salt – but you may not, so be careful. Finally, melt in the remaining butter.

Serve in bowls topped with grated Cheddar, some chopped parsley, black pepper and a hunk of bread on the side. Perfect for breakfast, lunch and dinner!

GAME STEW
with cranberries and rhubarb

This stew is inspired by the food of Persia, where rhubarb can be stewed with meat to create a sweet and sour dish. Spices reminiscent of the East are also included here to make a delicious dish rich with game that is softened by the acidity in the cranberries and rhubarb. Try to use really red rhubarb; the dish will look stunning.

Serves 4

3 tbsp olive oil
900g mixed game (venison, pigeon, pheasant, rabbit, duck), cut into 3–4cm pieces
2 red onions, finely sliced
3 garlic cloves, finely chopped
2 bay leaves
1 cinnamon stick, broken in two
2 pinches of freshly ground nutmeg
2 pinches of ground cloves

75g dried cranberries
350ml red wine
(Pinot noir works well as it's not too heavy)
100ml chicken stock
2–3 tbsp redcurrant jelly
200g rhubarb, cut into 2cm pieces
salt and freshly ground black pepper

To serve:
3 tbsp roughly chopped fresh parsley

Preheat the oven to 160°C/325°F/Fan 150°C/gas mark 3. Heat the oil in a heavy based, flameproof casserole dish that has a lid, on a medium heat, then brown the game for 3–4 minutes in batches, seasoning with black pepper as you go. Once browned, transfer the pieces to a bowl.

Add the onions to the pan, adding a little more oil and a splash of water if it's a bit dry and the onions seem to be sticking to the pan too much. Cook gently for 20 minutes until the onions are very soft, their juices have reduced, and they are sweet to the taste.

Add the garlic, bay leaves, cinnamon, nutmeg, ground cloves and the cranberries to the pan and cook for a couple of minutes. Then add the wine and stock, 2 tablespoons of the redcurrant jelly, a few pinches of salt and some black pepper. Return the browned meat to the pan and bring the stew to simmering point on the stove. Cover with the lid and transfer to the oven and cook for 1½ hours or until the meat is tender.

Take the dish out of the oven and stir in the chopped rhubarb. Pop the stew back in the oven and cook for about 10 minutes with the lid on still, to allow the fruit to cook through. You want the rhubarb to stay in whole pieces rather than completely break down. Taste for acidity and saltiness; if your rhubarb was very sour, you'll need to mix in the extra tablespoon of redcurrant jelly. Add a little more salt as well if you think it needs it.

Sprinkle with chopped parsley just before serving.

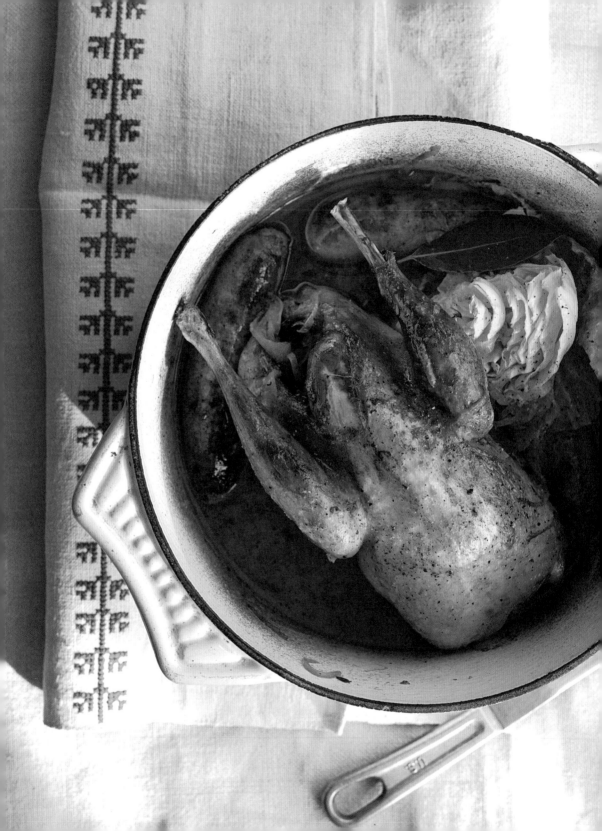

POT ROAST PHEASANT
with sausages, cabbage and ale

I love the way the cabbage in this recipe becomes all juicy and rich thanks to the tightly packed leaves that trap all the flavour inside.

Serves 4

2 tbsp olive oil
25g butter
4 coarse-cut sausages (about 250g), ideally Cumberland in traditional sausage format – but not big coils
2 pheasants (about 500g each)
salt and freshly ground black pepper

1 onion, finely sliced
4 sprigs of thyme
2 bay leaves
3 garlic cloves, finely chopped
1 small Savoy cabbage, outer leaves removed
400ml English amber ale

Preheat the oven to 160°C/325°F/Fan 150°C/gas mark 3. Heat the oil and butter in a large casserole dish that has a lid and is big enough to hold your pheasants. Once hot, gently brown the sausages for 5–7 minutes until golden on all sides, then transfer them to a plate and set aside to keep warm.

Next, season the pheasants with salt and black pepper and gently brown them in the casserole dish, turning after 3 or so minutes so all sides are nicely coloured. It should take 10–12 minutes to brown the birds – try to get a really nice golden colour. Once browned, set them aside with the sausages.

Now add the sliced onion, thyme sprigs, bay leaves and garlic to the pan. Cook gently for about 10 minutes until the onions are soft.

Meanwhile, quarter the cabbage, trimming back the tough stems but leaving enough to ensure the quarters don't fall apart.

Once the onion has softened, add the cabbage quarters to the pan followed by the ale and some grinds of black pepper. Return the pheasants to the pan along with the browned sausages and bring the ale to simmering point. Cover the pan with its lid and pop in the oven for about 40 minutes until the birds are tender (or longer if you've bought bigger birds).

Remove the cooked birds, sausages and cabbage to a serving plate and cover with foil to keep warm. Put the casserole dish on the hob and cook on a high heat for 5–10 minutes to reduce the juices to a sauce consistency. Taste for seasoning, adding a little more salt and black pepper if you think it needs it.

Serve with some boiled new potatoes or simply a generous quantity of crusty bread.

SPICED DUCK POT ROAST
with red cabbage and grapes

Braised red cabbage goes fantastically well with duck so I decided to combine the two in this spiced sweet and sour pot roast. Go for duck legs and thighs rather than breast as these will stay more juicy and succulent. This dish is perfect at any time of the year but the delicious smells coming from your oven will make you think it's Christmas!

Serves 4

400g red cabbage, tough core removed and sliced into long strips
2 onions, thinly sliced
3 garlic cloves, finely chopped
1 Granny Smith apple, peeled, cored and roughly chopped
180g seedless grapes
50g dried cranberries (or 65g fresh)

1 pinch each of ground cloves, cinnamon and nutmeg
100ml red wine
3 tbsp sherry vinegar
salt and freshly ground black pepper
4 duck legs, thighs attached
(about 200g each)

Preheat the oven to 160°C/325°F/Fan 150°C/gas mark 3. In a large, flameproof casserole dish that has a lid, mix together all the ingredients except the duck along with a couple of generous pinches of salt and a few grinds of a pepper mill. Put the dish on a low heat on the hob just to get things bubbling, then pop in the oven, lid on, for 1½ hours. Give everything a stir a couple of times during the cooking time.

Meanwhile, trim the duck legs of any excess skin or fat and score the surface of the skin with a sharp knife, taking care not to pierce the flesh, only the skin. (Scoring helps the fat to be released and encourages browning.) Season the duck with salt and black pepper and in a dry non-stick frying pan, brown the pieces of duck on a medium heat, skin-side down. Don't crowd the pan, so do it in batches if you have to. The duck will release a lot of fat, so drain it off as you go (keep it in the fridge for delicious roast potatoes) and continue browning for about 7 minutes until most of the fat has rendered and the skin side is a deep golden brown colour. Quickly seal the other side for a couple of minutes and set aside on a plate.

After the cabbage has been cooking for 1½ hours, remove it from the oven and place the browned duck pieces skin-side up on top of the red cabbage mixture. Place the dish back in the oven, covered, for a further 1½ hours until most of the liquid in the pot has reduced. Don't be afraid to give the cabbage under the duck a little stir or shake a few times during cooking.

After enjoying the aromas for a few hours, you'll be left with delicious sweet and sour red cabbage and meltingly soft duck on top. Add a little more salt to the cabbage if you think it needs it. Serve with some crunchy sautéed potatoes (see page 148).

BEEF IN ALE
with horseradish and Stilton dumplings

This good old British stew (page 41) is always a winner and, conveniently, very easy to make. The dumplings are, of course, optional, but a real treat.

Serves 4

3 tbsp olive oil
900g beef chuck steak, cut into 3–4cm pieces
2 onions, roughly chopped
1 tbsp plain flour
500ml Guinness or dark ale
1 tsp English mustard (made from English mustard powder)
2 carrots, peeled and chopped into large chunks
2 parsnips, peeled and chopped into large chunks
400g tin chopped tomatoes
2 bay leaves
salt and freshly ground black pepper

For the dumplings:
200g self-raising flour
100g vegetable or beef suet
½ tsp salt
50g Stilton, crumbled
1 tbsp finely chopped parsley
1 tbsp hot horseradish (from a jar)
150ml water

To serve:
2 tbsp chopped fresh parsley

Preheat the oven to 160°C/325°F/Fan 150°C/gas mark 3. Heat the oil in a large, heavy based, flameproof casserole dish that has a lid and brown the beef pieces for 3–4 minutes in batches. Once the meat is well browned, transfer to a bowl.

Add the onions to the pan and cook gently for about 10 minutes until soft and transparent, adding a little more oil and a splash of water if the pan seems dry. Once the onions have softened, add the flour and stir well. After a couple of minutes, pour in the Guinness or dark ale, scraping off any bits from the base of the pan as these give a good flavour to your stew. Stir in the mustard before dropping in the carrots, parsnips, tomatoes and bay leaves.

Return the browned beef and any juices that may have collected to the pan and season with a few pinches of salt and some black pepper. Bring everything to simmering point then cover with the lid and cook in the oven for 1½–2 hours or until the beef is lovely and tender and the sauce has thickened. Feel free to cook it on a low heat on the hob if you prefer.

In the meantime, make the dumplings. In a bowl, mix together the flour, suet and salt using your fingertips to break up the suet – you can do this in a food processor too, of course. Next add the crumbled Stilton and the parsley to the bowl (remove the mixture from the processor if you've used one). Combine the hot horseradish with the water and mix this into the dry ingredients, bringing it together with your hands until you've got a good dough consistency. Then, using your hands, roll the dough into 8–10 balls and set aside, covered, to prevent them drying out.

When the beef is soft and tender, taste the stew and check it for seasoning as it's going to be hard to do this once the dumplings are on top. Once you're happy with the flavour, drop the dumplings on top, cover with the lid and return to the oven or set on a low heat on the hob for 30 minutes.

After this time, the dumplings will have puffed up, so remove the lid and raise the temperature of the oven to 180°C/350°F/Fan 160°C/gas mark 4. (If you've been cooking on the hob until now you need to do the next bit in the oven or under a grill.) Cook again until the dumplings have developed a crust on top. Scatter some chopped parsley over and serve in bowls with some creamy mashed potato.

LANCASHIRE HOTPOT

Another British classic cooked in the oven with an addictive crunchy potato topping (page 40, top).

Serves 4

3 tbsp olive oil
900g lamb shoulder,
trimmed of as much fat as possible
and cut into 2–3cm pieces
salt and freshly ground black pepper
4 lamb's kidneys (optional),
halved, fatty core removed with scissors
and cut into pieces
40g butter
2 onions, roughly chopped

1 tbsp flour
500ml hot water
1½ tbsp Worcestershire sauce
2 bay leaves
2 sprigs of thyme
850g potatoes, peeled and cut
into 1cm slices
freshly grated nutmeg
2 carrots, peeled and roughly chopped

Preheat the oven to 160°C/325°F/Fan 150°C/gas mark 3. In a non-stick frying pan, heat the oil and brown the lamb in batches, seasoning the pieces with black pepper as you go and setting them aside once browned. Next, brown the kidneys, if using, and set aside with the lamb.

Add half the butter to the frying pan and gently brown the onions for 10–12 minutes. Once golden at the edges, add the flour and cook for another couple of minutes, stirring to incorporate. Then add the water and Worcestershire sauce, the bay leaves and the thyme. Season with salt and black pepper. Bring to the boil and cook for a couple of minutes to create a thin gravy.

Next, smear some of the remaining butter around the base and sides of a deep casserole dish that's about 30cm wide. Put a layer of potatoes over the base and season them with salt, black pepper and a little freshly grated nutmeg. On top of the potatoes layer up the meat, kidneys (if using) and carrots and then pour the gravy on top. Finish with the remaining potatoes to as a final layer. Dot the top with the remaining butter and season with some more salt, black pepper and nutmeg. Cover with the lid and cook in the oven for 2 hours.

Remove the lid, increase your oven temperature to 190°C/375°F/Fan 180°C/gas mark 5 and continue cooking for a further 30 minutes to brown the potatoes and reduce the liquid a little. If you want a really crunchy topping, simply pop it under the grill for a few minutes.

IRISH STEW

A stew cookbook really couldn't exist without a good old Irish stew. The following recipe certainly isn't the only way to make this grandfather of stews, in fact there are countless variations. I've chosen to use lamb but some people prefer beef; some add turnips and parsnips, I've just gone for carrots and potatoes. Some cook it in the oven, layered like a Lancashire hotpot, but I like it on the hob just as my mum did it when I was a kid – and here it is.

Serves 4–6

1.2kg middle neck lamb chops, trim off as much fat as possible and reserve
salt and freshly ground black pepper
2 bay leaves
4 tbsp pearl barley
2 onions, sliced
2 garlic cloves, roughly chopped
3 carrots, roughly chopped (keep them chunky)
500g floury potatoes, peeled and cut into roast potato-sized chunks

To serve:
chopped fresh parsley

Heat a few of the fat trimmings from the lamb in a large non-stick frying pan. Once they've melted, season the chops with salt and black pepper, brown them on both sides for 2–3 minutes in batches, then transfer them to a deep, heavy based pan.

Once all the chops have been browned, cover them with cold water in the deep pan. Pop in the bay leaves and bring to the boil. Reduce the heat and simmer gently, skimming off any fat and scum that rises to the top using a metal spoon.

After 30 minutes, in a separate small saucepan, cover the barley with cold water and bring to the boil. Once boiling, drain and rinse in cold water before adding to the simmering lamb.

Once the lamb has been cooking for a total of 1½ hours, add the onions, garlic, carrots, potatoes, a few generous pinches of salt and some grinds of black pepper. Cook for a further 30 minutes before tasting for seasoning. At this point I like to crush a few of the potatoes into the liquid to thicken it slightly.

Serve in big bowls sprinkled with chopped parsley.

RICH OXTAIL STEW

The first time I made oxtail stew I didn't have enough wine in the house, so I thought, 'What the hell, I'll add some beer as well and see what happens'. The result was fantastic and I've been cooking it that way ever since.

A Gary Rhodes recipe introduced me to the idea of adding peeled and chopped tomatoes as well as some freshly cooked vegetables to the sieved and reduced sauce. This not only gives the stew a lighter touch but also adds colour and texture.

When buying oxtails, try to get the thick end of the tails – these have more meat and less bone so are more satisfying. Oxtail is surprisingly fatty, so trim off as much fat as possible from the pieces, getting in with your knife as best you can.

Serves 4

2kg oxtails, trimmed of fat and cut into 4–5cm pieces
salt and freshly ground black pepper
3 tbsp olive oil
2 carrots, roughly chopped
2 celery sticks, roughly chopped
½ leek, roughly chopped
2 onions, roughly chopped
3 sprigs of thyme
3 bay leaves
2 garlic cloves, roughly chopped
500ml red wine
500ml beer
1 litre beef stock
400g tin chopped tomatoes

To finish the stew:
4 tomatoes
1 carrot, finely chopped
1 leek, finely chopped, white section only
2 celery sticks, finely chopped

To serve:
chopped fresh parsley

Preheat the oven to 160°C/325°F/Fan 150°C/gas mark 3. Season the oxtail with salt and black pepper. Heat the oil in a large, flameproof casserole dish that has a lid (it needs to be able to fit 2 litres of liquid plus lots of veg and oxtails, so the bigger the better) and brown the oxtails in a couple of batches on all sides. You'll need to spend 2–3 minutes on each side to get a good colour. Transfer each batch to a bowl and set aside and keep warm.

Add the carrots, celery, leek and onions to the pan with the thyme and bay leaves. Gently cook these for 10–12 minutes on a moderate heat until the onions have softened and are starting to brown at the edges. Now add the garlic and cook for a couple more minutes.

Pour in the wine, beer, stock, chopped tomatoes and some black pepper. Don't add any salt yet as the sauce will be reduced later which will intensify all the flavours – we'll only add salt at the end. Now return the browned oxtail and any collected juices to the pan. Bring the stew to simmering point and pop the dish in the oven with the lid on for 3½ hours.

The oxtail will now be extremely tender; remove the pieces carefully from the pan and set aside on a plate. Sieve the sauce into a bowl using the back of a wooden spoon to push through all the liquid you can from the cooked vegetables. Discard the drained vegetables then return the sieved liquid to the dish and reduce it until it's the consistency of single cream and rich in flavour. This may take up to 20 minutes. Now add a little salt if you feel it needs it.

Meanwhile, with the point of a knife, make a cross at the base of each tomato. Put the tomatoes in a heatproof bowl and pour over boiling water until they are submerged, then leave them for 1 minute. Drain and cool them under cold water. The skins should now slip off. Cut the tomatoes into quarters and remove the seeds, then chop the flesh into small pieces.

Put all the finely chopped vegetables into a small saucepan. Add 2 tablespoons of water and cook on high heat, with a lid on, for 3–4 minutes until the vegetables have softened slightly.

Once the meaty sauce has fully reduced and you're about to serve the dish, add the cooked vegetables and the oxtails back to the sauce to heat through. Then gently mix in the peeled and chopped tomatoes.

Serve with mashed potato and sprinkle with a little chopped parsley.

Tip – You can make everything a day ahead up until the point of cooking the diced vegetables and preparing the tomatoes. Before serving, simply warm the stew through and then stir in the veg.

BEEF WITH BEETROOT AND STILTON

The addition of creamy Stilton gives a rich saltiness to this stew.

Serves 4

2 tbsp olive oil
900g chuck steak, cut into 3–4cm pieces
salt and freshly ground black pepper
2 onions, roughly chopped
2 celery sticks, roughly chopped
3 garlic cloves, finely chopped
2 bay leaves
1 tsp caraway seeds
250ml red wine
150ml beef stock
2 tbsp balsamic vinegar
400g tin chopped tomatoes
350g raw beetroot, peeled and cut into 1½–2cm pieces

To serve:
150g Stilton

Preheat the oven to 160°C/325°F/Fan 150°C/gas mark 3, or you can use your hob. Heat the oil in a heavy based, flameproof casserole dish that has a lid and brown the meat for 3–4 minutes in batches, seasoning with salt and black pepper as you go. Transfer the browned meat to a bowl and set aside.

Once you've browned all the meat, add the onions, celery and garlic to the pan along with the bay leaves and caraway seeds. Add a splash more oil if you need to and a sprinkling of water if the pan is too dry. Cook on a gentle heat for about 10 minutes or until the onions have softened.

Next add the wine, stock, vinegar, tomatoes and some salt and black pepper. Bring to simmering point before finally adding the beetroot, browned beef and any collected juices to the pan.

Cover with a lid and cook in the oven or on the hob for about 2 hours until the beef is lovely and tender. If you think the sauce isn't looking thick enough, remove the lid for the last 30 minutes.

Stir 100g of the Stilton through the stew just before serving and taste for seasoning. When you're happy with the flavour, crumble a little more cheese on top to serve. This is perfect with some creamy mashed potato.

PORK
with apples and prunes

Apples and prunes go so well together, even in a stew!

Serves 4

2 tbsp olive oil
100g smoked lardons
900g lean pork shoulder,
cut into 3–4cm cubes
salt and freshly ground black pepper
2 onions, roughly chopped
1 leek, finely sliced
2 carrots, peeled and cut into 2cm chunks
2 garlic cloves, finely chopped
2 bay leaves
2 tsp chopped sage leaves

5 tbsp brandy
250ml apple juice
1 tbsp cider vinegar
200ml hot chicken stock
12 pitted prunes
25g butter
2 Cox apples, peeled, cored and
quartered, or 1 Bramley apple,
peeled and cut into large chunks
(Bramley apples will give you a more
acidic stew which I think works well)

Preheat the oven to 160°C/325°F/Fan 150°C/gas mark 3. Heat the oil in a heavy based, flameproof casserole dish that has a lid, add the lardons and brown gently for about 5 minutes. Remove with a slotted spoon to a plate. Next brown the pork pieces in batches for 3–4 minutes, seasoning with black pepper as you go. Once browned, reserve alongside the lardons.

Add the onions to the pan along with the leek and a splash more oil and a little water if the pan is too dry. Scrape off any bits from the base of the pan and cook gently for 5 minutes before adding the carrots, garlic, bay leaves and sage. Cook gently for a further 5 minutes.

Meanwhile, melt the butter in a separate frying pan and fry the apple gently for 5–8 minutes to brown them slightly around the edges, turning them halfway through. Take care not to burn the butter.

Add the brandy to the vegetables in the casserole dish and cook for 2–3 minutes to drive off the alcohol before pouring in the apple juice, cider vinegar, stock and some salt and black pepper. Return the pork and lardons to the dish along with the prunes. Once the apples are nicely browned, add them to the stew along with the butter they were cooked in and pop the casserole in the oven for 2 hours.

The apples will break down thickening the sauce, giving it a fruity richness. Taste for seasoning. If the apple juice you used was particularly sweet, you may need to add a touch more vinegar.

Serve with brown rice.

VENISON
with chestnuts, port and orange

This stew looks and tastes like autumn.

Serves 4

900g stewing venison,
cut into 3–4cm pieces
salt and freshly ground black pepper
2 tbsp sunflower oil
2 onions, roughly chopped
2 carrots, peeled and roughly chopped
2 celery sticks, roughly chopped
2 garlic cloves, finely chopped
3–4 sprigs of thyme

2 bay leaves
½ tbsp juniper berries, crushed
1 tbsp plain flour
juice of 1 orange, grated zest of ½ orange
250ml port
150ml beef stock
100g chestnut mushrooms, halved,
or oyster mushrooms, torn into pieces
200g cooked and peeled chestnuts

Preheat the oven to 160°C/325°F/Fan 150°C/gas mark 3. Season the venison with black pepper. Heat the oil in a deep, flameproof casserole dish that has a lid and brown the venison for 3–4 minutes in batches. Add a little more oil after the first couple of batches if you need to. Once the meat is browned, set aside in a bowl.

Add the onions to the pan, and soften on a gentle heat for 10–15 minutes, scraping any bits that may have got stuck on the bottom of the pan. (These bits really do add flavour to stews so you want to scrape them off rather than give them the opportunity to burn on the base of the pan.) If the pan feels a little dry, add a drizzle more oil and a splash of water.

Once the onions have softened, add the carrots, celery, garlic, thyme, bay leaves and crushed juniper berries. Continue to cook gently for a further 10 minutes.

Add the flour, stirring to combine well. After a couple of minutes, add the orange juice and zest, port, stock, mushrooms and some salt and black pepper. Now return the browned venison along with any juices that may have collected to the pan. Bring to the boil then cover with a lid and pop in the oven for 1½ hours.

Stir in the chestnuts and return the dish to the oven. Depending on the venison, the stew will need a further 30 minutes–1 hour to cook through and it is ready when the venison has completely tenderised.

PUY LENTIL, BEETROOT, PECAN AND GOATS' CHEESE STEW

This vegetarian stew is just as delicious served at room temperature.

Serves 4–6

50g butter
1 carrot, cut into ½cm pieces
1 celery stick, cut into ½cm pieces
½ leek, outer leaves removed
and finely chopped
1 onion, finely chopped
½ fennel bulb, finely chopped
2 garlic cloves, finely chopped
1 tsp cumin seeds
1 bay leaf
125g chestnut mushrooms, quartered
200ml white wine
200g puy lentils

600ml hot vegetable stock
salt and freshly ground black pepper
75g goats' cheese, crumbled

For the beetroot:
300g small raw beetroot,
peeled and quartered
2 tsp olive oil

To serve:
75g goats' cheese, crumbled
75g pecan nuts
chopped fresh parsley

Preheat the oven to 190°C/375°F/Fan 180°C/gas mark 5. Melt the butter in a flameproof casserole dish that has a lid. Throw the carrot, celery, leek, onion, fennel, garlic, cumin seeds and bay leaf into the pan and gently cook for about 15 minutes until the onion has softened and the carrots have started to soften.

Meanwhile, in a bowl, coat the beetroot pieces in the olive oil and season with salt and black pepper. Spread them out on a baking tray and cook in the oven for 30–40 minutes until soft and caramelising slightly at the edges.

Once the vegetables have been cooking in the pan for 15 minutes, add the chestnut mushrooms and cook gently for a further 5 minutes. Pour in the white wine and boil rapidly for a couple of minutes to drive off the alcohol. Rinse the lentils before adding them to the vegetables followed by the stock and a few good grinds of black pepper.

Cover with a lid and place the dish in the oven for 30 minutes until the lentils are cooked and the liquid has reduced considerably.

Finish the stew by stirring in a few pinches of salt and the goats' cheese so that it melts gently into the lentils. Taste for seasoning and add more salt or black pepper if you think it needs it.

Serve the lentils in bowls topped with the cooked beetroot, and the goats' cheese, pecan nuts and chopped parsley.

EUROPE

CATALAN FISH STEW

Ground nuts enrich the smoky tomatoey sauce of this fish stew. The sauce can be made ahead and then the fish added at the last minute just before you want to serve it. Makes life easy!

Serves 4

125g blanched almonds or hazelnuts
4 tbsp extra virgin olive oil
6 garlic cloves, finely sliced
½ tsp crushed dried chillies
1 bay leaf
1 onion, finely sliced
1½ red peppers, finely sliced lengthways
1 tsp sweet smoked paprika
2 pinches of saffron strands
45ml brandy
150g chopped tomatoes

275ml white wine
salt and freshly ground black pepper
700g firm, thick white fish fillets
(monkfish, haddock or cod),
cut into 5–7cm pieces
4 large raw prawns, shells on
12 mussels, scrubbed and cleaned
12 clams, scrubbed and cleaned
chopped fresh parsley
juice of ½ lemon

Begin by toasting the nuts. Scatter them over a baking tray and set it under a medium grill for 5–7 minutes until turning golden. Stir them a couple of times so that they brown evenly and make sure you keep an eye on them otherwise they'll burn. Allow to cool and then grind the nuts using a mortar and pestle or a food processor. They don't have to be finely ground, but try to avoid any large lumps.

In a wide, non-stick frying pan that has a lid, heat the oil and gently fry the garlic, dried chillies and bay leaf for 2–3 minutes until the garlic starts to turn golden. Lower the heat and add the onion and red peppers. Gently cook for 15–20 minutes until the vegetables are very soft.

Stir in the smoked paprika and saffron and continue to cook for a couple of minutes so the spices can release their flavours. Add the brandy and boil for a minute or so until nearly evaporated and then add the tomatoes. Cook gently for a further 5 minutes before adding the wine, a few pinches of salt and some black pepper. Cook gently for a further 7–10 minutes until the tomatoes have completely broken down.

Lower the heat and add the ground nuts to the dish. Season the pieces of fish with a little salt before pushing them into the sauce, along with the prawns, mussels and clams. Cover with a lid. Cook gently for 5–7 minutes until the fish is just cooked and the shells of the mussels and clams have opened. Discard any shells that have not opened. Test for seasoning before gently stirring the parsley through and squeezing the lemon juice over the dish.

Serve in bowls with crusty bread.

CUTTLEFISH BRAISED IN RED WINE, CLOVES AND BAY LEAVES

This dish is inspired by a chance meeting in my local fishmonger's on Green Lanes. I was in the process of deciding what to buy and started speaking to a Greek lady next to me who was buying some cuttlefish. I asked her what she was making and she described how she was going to cook the cuttlefish gently in red wine with garlic, some cloves, cinnamon and bay leaves. It sounded delicious so she wrote down her recipe and here it is!

Cuttlefish is completely neglected in the UK but it's fantastic. Because it's quite meaty and the flesh is pretty thick, it lends itself perfectly to long slow cooking. Ask your fishmonger to clean the cuttlefish and to reserve a small sack of its ink, which you can use in the recipe to give an amazing black colour to the dish. If you can't find cuttlefish, use squid instead and reduce the cooking time by 20 minutes.

Serves 4

4 tbsp extra virgin olive oil
2 onions, finely sliced
8 peppercorns
3 bay leaves
3 cloves
1 cinnamon stick, broken in two
4 garlic cloves, thinly sliced
1kg prepared cuttlefish,
cut into 1cm strips

200 ml red wine
2 tsp red wine vinegar
¼ tsp cuttlefish ink (optional)
salt
juice of 1 lemon

To serve:
2–3 tbsp chopped fresh parsley
lemon wedges

Preheat the oven to 160°C/325°F/Fan 150°C/gas mark 3, or you can use the hob if you prefer. Heat the oil in a heavy based, flameproof casserole dish that has a lid, then add the onions, peppercorns, bay leaves, cloves and cinnamon stick and cook gently for about 10 minutes until the onions have softened. Then add the garlic and cook gently for a further 5 minutes.

Add the cuttlefish pieces to the pan and cook for about 5 more minutes until the flesh has turned opaque. Then add the red wine, vinegar and the cuttlefish ink, if using. Bring to simmering point, season with some salt, cover the dish with the lid and pop it in the oven or on a low heat on the hob for 1 hour until the cuttlefish is tender.

Season with a few pinches of salt, squeeze in the lemon juice, sprinkle with chopped parsley and serve with lemon wedges on some plain bulgur wheat or rice.

CATAPLANA
Portuguese seafood stew

A Portuguese friend of my mum always raved about *cataplanas*, the Portuguese one-pot where all the ingredients are layered and then cooked together (apart from the fish, which goes in at the end). A cataplana is actually a type of cooking pot made of copper that has an extremely tight-fitting lid. I'm assuming you don't have one and aren't about to buy one, so you'll be pleased to know that you can make a cataplana in any deep pot that has a tight-fitting lid.

Serves 4

4 tbsp extra virgin olive oil
500g new potatoes, peeled and cut into ½cm slices
salt and freshly ground black pepper
2 sprigs of fresh thyme
2 bay leaves
½ mild red chilli, deseeded and thinly sliced (add the whole chilli if you want more spice)
2 large garlic cloves, finely chopped
1 red pepper, quartered lengthways then sliced into 5mm strips
1 onion, very thinly sliced

100g chorizo, thinly sliced
200g ripe tomatoes, cut into ½cm slices
100ml white wine
100ml fish stock
700g firm white fish fillets, cut into 5–7cm chunks (monkfish, red mullet, cod, coley – you can also add king prawns or squid rings)
200g mussels, cleaned and scrubbed
200g clams, cleaned and scrubbed

To serve:
chopped fresh parsley

Pour half the olive oil evenly over the base of a deep, flameproof pan that has a lid and cover with the potatoes. Season them with some salt and black pepper, then throw in the sprigs of thyme and bay leaves, followed by the chilli and garlic. Try to scatter them evenly over the potatoes.

Next, arrange the red pepper and onion slices on top, followed by the chorizo and tomatoes. Sprinkle the whole lot with the remaining olive oil and season with more salt and black pepper. Finally, pour over the wine and the fish stock.

Cover the pot with foil before covering with the lid – you want a really tight fit so that all the ingredients cook in their own steam. Cook on top of the stove on a low heat for 30 minutes.

Season the fish pieces with some salt, then remove the lid and the foil and place the fish, mussels and clams on top of all the vegetables. Cover again with the foil and lid and cook for a further 15 minutes until the mussels have opened fully and the fish is just cooked. Discard any shells that have not opened.

Sprinkle with chopped parsley and serve.

SALT COD, CHICKPEA AND CHERRY TOMATO STEW

Salt cod is eaten all over the Mediterranean and in South America. Salting fish was *the* preservation method before refrigeration; it can vary from pieces that are as hard as wood, which last many years, to the softer, less dry variety. For this dish, try to get the softer one. Here the salt cod is cooked gently with chickpeas, a great partner to the fish as they balance the saltiness, while cherry tomatoes add fruitiness to the whole dish.

Remember to start this the day before you want to eat it, as you have to soak the cod in water overnight to remove excess salt.

Serves 4

450g salt cod fillet
5 tbsp extra virgin olive oil
1 onion, thinly sliced
1 red pepper, quartered and thinly sliced
2 pinches of dried crushed chilli
4 garlic cloves, thinly sliced
2 bay leaves
½ tsp sweet smoked paprika
175ml white wine

2 tins cooked chickpeas,
rinsed and drained
250g cherry tomatoes, halved
juice of 1 lemon
4 tbsp roughly chopped fresh parsley
freshly ground black pepper

To serve:
extra virgin olive oil

Rinse the cod in cold water to remove any excess salt and then soak it in a bowl of water for 24 hours. Change the water a couple of times during this time. The next day, remove the skin from the salt cod with a fish-filleting knife or by carefully pulling it away from the flesh. Then cut it into 4–5cm pieces.

Heat the oil in a wide frying pan that has a lid. Cook the onion, red pepper, chilli, garlic and bay leaves very slowly for 20 minutes until the vegetables are very soft and the onion is starting to turn a little golden.

Add the smoked paprika and cook gently for a couple of minutes before adding the wine. Boil rapidly for a couple of minutes to drive off the alcohol, then add the fish to the pan. Cover with the lid and cook for a couple of minutes, then stir in the chickpeas and halved tomatoes. Replace the lid and cook for a further 3–5 minutes. You want the salt cod to break up a little into the chickpeas and the tomatoes to just start releasing their juices.

Finish the dish by stirring through the lemon juice and the chopped parsley, then grind over some black pepper and drizzle a little more olive oil on top.

Serve simply with crusty bread and a salad.

BOUILLABAISSE

This is the quintessential French fish stew served with croutons and piquant sauce – *rouille* – made from chilli pepper, red pepper and olive oil.

As always, it's essential you use really fresh fish for the stew. Feel free to ask your fishmonger to skin your fillets. However, keeping the skin on will prevent the fillets breaking up during cooking and can make it look quite stunning – red mullet, for example, has a beautiful shiny red skin which it seems a shame to remove! Ask your fishmonger to give you the bones so you can add real flavour to the stew.

Serves 4

6 tbsp extra virgin olive oil
½ bulb fennel, finely chopped
1 celery stick, finely diced
½ onion, finely diced
7 garlic cloves, roughly chopped
2 sprigs of fresh thyme
2 good pinches of dried and crushed chillies
2 tsp fennel seeds
2 bay leaves
4 pieces of orange zest, peeled with a potato peeler
2 pinches of saffron
8 large prawns, heads removed and reserved
2 chopped ripe tomatoes
1 glass white wine (about 175ml)
1 litre boiling water
700g white fish fillets (sea bass, red mullet, monkfish, gurnard, John Dory), bones retained and skin removed or not, depending on your preference, cut into 5–7cm pieces or smaller if your fillets are very thick

200g clams
200g mussels, scrubbed and cleaned
salt and freshly ground black pepper

For the rouille:
2 red peppers
6 garlic cloves, unpeeled
1 red chilli, deseeded and chopped
6 tbsp olive oil
2 tbsp white breadcrumbs
salt

Croutons:
8 x 1cm thick slices French bread
olive oil

To serve:
roughly chopped fresh flat leaf parsley

Heat the olive oil in a saucepan that has a lid and is big enough to hold all your fish and shellfish. Throw in the fennel, celery, onion, garlic, thyme, chillies, fennel seeds, bay leaves, orange zest and saffron as well as the prawn heads. Cook gently for 10 minutes. Give the prawn heads a squash from time to time so any juices come out into and mix with the cooking vegetables.

After 10 minutes, add the tomatoes and cook for another couple of minutes before adding the wine. Raise the heat and boil off the alcohol for about 2 minutes or so. Add the fish bones and the boiling water and simmer gently for 20 minutes.

Meanwhile, make the rouille. Simply cut the red peppers in half and remove the seeds. Place them skin-side up on a baking tray with the garlic cloves and put them under a hot grill for 10 minutes until the skin of the peppers has turned black in patches and blistered. Allow the peppers to cool a little before removing the skin and chopping into small pieces. Remove the skins from the grilled garlic cloves and blitz these in a blender with the grilled pepper and fresh red chilli. Then slowly add the olive oil, 1 tablespoon at a time, continuing to blitz all the time. Once incorporated, stir through the breadcrumbs and season with salt.

Preheat the oven to 190°C/375°F/Fan 180°C/gas mark 5. Now make the croutons. Simply dip both sides of the slices of bread in olive oil and bake in the oven for 10–15 minutes until crisp and dry. These can be kept in an airtight container for several hours or even days without going soggy.

Now back to the pot of bones and vegetables. Once everything has been simmering for 20 minutes, strain the whole lot through a sieve into a large bowl, pushing it with the back of a wooden spoon to make sure you get all the juices and flavour out of the vegetables, bones and prawn heads.

Return the strained liquid to the pan and bring back to simmering point. Add the prawns and fish fillets and cook very gently for about a minute before adding the clams and mussels. Cover with the lid and cook for 2–3 minutes until the shells have opened and the fish is cooked. As soon as the seafood is cooked, remove to a flat platter and cover with foil to keep warm. Discard any shells that have not opened.

Now turn up the heat and boil the liquid for a couple of minutes to reduce it slightly. Taste the soup, adding salt if you think it needs it. It should have a hint of chilli, be fragrant with saffron and have a lovely taste of the sea.

Spoon piles of fish and seafood into bowls and ladle around the soup. Serve sprinkled with some chopped parsley and the croutons with a bowl of rouille alongside.

Tip – You can cook everything ahead of schedule up to the point of adding fish to the strained cooking liquor.

POLLO AL AJILLO
Chicken cooked with garlic, bay leaves and white wine

I've eaten *pollo al ajillo* so many times in Spain but it's been cooked differently every time. This way of cooking it is my favourite and the recipe below is adapted from one by Sam and Sam Clark of Moro, in London.

Serves 4

5 tbsp olive oil
1 head of garlic, separated
into cloves (unpeeled)
6 bay leaves
8 chicken thighs (about 1kg in total)
salt and freshly ground black pepper

200ml white wine
100ml water
juice of 1 or 2 lemons

To serve:
chopped fresh parsley

Heat the olive oil in a pan that's wide enough to hold all the chicken thighs in one layer and has a lid. Once hot, add the garlic cloves and bay leaves and cook gently for a couple of minutes.

Next, season the chicken thighs with salt and black pepper and add to the pan, skin-side down. Fry them gently for 7–10 minutes until the skin is golden and crisp. Turn the thighs over and cook for a couple more minutes on the other side. You may need to fry the chicken in batches to prevent it steaming instead of browning.

Return all the chicken to the pan, add the wine and cook on a high heat for a couple of minutes to drive off the alcohol. Add the water and a little more salt and black pepper, and once the liquid is boiling again, lower the heat. The oil, wine and water will have now emulsified to create a creamy consistency.

Cover the pan with its lid and cook gently for 25–30 minutes until the chicken is ready. Give the pan regular shakes during the cooking time to prevent anything sticking.

Stir in the juice from one of the lemons and taste the sauce. If you feel it needs to be a little more lemony, add the juice from the second lemon. Add some more salt, too, if you think it needs it.

Sprinkle with chopped parsley and serve with hunks of bread to mop up the sauce. When you're tucking in, don't forget to squeeze out the cooked garlic from their protective skins – they are delicious.

COQ AU VIN

Another rustic French classic that, I think, can find itself unfairly relegated to the back of the class. A bath of red wine, brandy, lardons, shallots, mushrooms and herbs is a great treat for a chicken! I remember having this for the first time in a rural French spa town on a summer holiday when I was a kid. We'd been driving for hours so the coq au vin was even more of a treat.

Serves 4

1 chicken (approx 1.6kg), cut into about 6 joints
(get your butcher to do this and ask him to reserve the carcass)

For the stock:
1 celery stick, broken into pieces
1 onion, cut into quarters
1 carrot, broken into pieces
a couple of parsley stalks
2 bay leaves
2 sprigs of thyme
a few peppercorns

For the stew:
60g butter
200g smoked lardons (try to buy ones about 1cm thick,
or buy a big piece of smoked bacon and cut it into small pieces)
salt and freshly ground black pepper
12 shallots
250g button mushrooms, cleaned and trimmed
2 tbsp plain flour
1 bottle red wine
4 tbsp brandy
3 garlic cloves, thinly sliced
2 sprigs of fresh thyme
2 bay leaves

Begin by making a light chicken stock. Put the chicken carcass in a large, deep saucepan that it will fit into with space to spare, completely cover the bones with cold water and throw in the celery, onion, carrot, parsley stalks, bay leaves, thyme and peppercorns. Bring to the boil, then simmer gently.

Melt half the butter in a heavy based, flameproof casserole dish and gently brown the lardons. When the edges are nicely caramelised, remove them with a slotted spoon and set aside in a bowl. Next, season the chicken joints with salt and black pepper and gently brown the pieces in the same pan (do this in batches if you need to) for 5–7 minutes until the skin side is golden brown. Once the pieces are browned, set them aside in the bowl with the lardons. Ensure the heat is not too high when browning the chicken otherwise the butter will burn.

Next, peel the shallots. The easiest way to do this is by dropping them into boiling water for 1 minute, then plunge them into cold water. The skins will slip off easily once you've removed the root.

Melt the remaining butter in the casserole dish and add the mushrooms and peeled shallots. After about 10 minutes, once they are nicely browned, remove with a slotted spoon to join the lardons and chicken. Add the flour to the casserole dish and mix together with the remaining fat in the pan. Cook on a low heat for a couple of minutes and incorporate all the flour into the fat to make a 'roux'. Cook for a couple of minutes before stirring in the wine (which will dissolve the roux) and then add the brandy, garlic, thyme and bay leaves.

Return the chicken, lardons, mushrooms and onions (and any tasty juices that may have collected) to the pan. Top up with the stock you've been making until the chicken is just covered and add a few pinches of salt and a few grinds of black pepper. Bring to simmering point and then very gently cook the chicken with the lid on for about 40 minutes–1 hour until it's tender (the older the chicken, the longer it will take to cook).

Once the chicken is tender, remove the pieces with a slotted spoon along with as many onions, mushrooms and lardons that you can fish out from the pan. Set aside all of this in a bowl, and cover it with tin foil to keep warm.

Turn up the heat and reduce the cooking liquor by about half until it thickens very slightly. Make sure you taste the sauce as you don't want it to be too strong – only add more salt once you're happy with the consistency. Then return the chicken, lardons, mushrooms and onions to the pan, warming through a little before serving with chunks of good crusty bread to mop up the delicious sauce.

CHICKEN AND SEAFOOD PAELLA

A paella (page 71) is certainly a one-pot wonder and comes in many guises. Ideally you'd have a *paellera*, a special paella pan, and a wood fire to cook this on, but realistically any wide and deep frying pan and a hob will do the trick.

I learnt this recipe during a working holiday in Spain as a student and have been perfecting it ever since. It's a real winner with my family and appears at key birthdays.

A quick note on paella rice – it's important to buy true Spanish paella rice to get an authentic dish as it creates just the right amount of stickiness. All paella rices will differ, however, so depending on the type you use, you may need a little more stock than this recipe calls for.

Serves 4

2 tbsp extra virgin olive oil
4 chicken thighs
(about 500g in total), skin on
1 onion, finely chopped
1 red pepper, quartered lengthways
and cut into 5mm thick slices
1 pinch of dried crushed chilli
2 bay leaves
100g mild chorizo, sliced
2 garlic cloves, chopped
150g squid, cleaned and sliced
a couple of pinches of saffron strands
1 tsp sweet smoked paprika

200g chopped tomatoes
250g paella rice (ideally *calasparra*)
600–650ml hot chicken stock
juice of ½ lemon
salt and freshly ground black pepper
8 mussels, scrubbed and cleaned
8 raw prawns, shells on
40g runner beans, chopped and cooked

To serve:
lemon wedges
chopped fresh parsley

Heat the oil in a wide and deep frying pan, then gently brown the chicken pieces, skin-side down, for 5–7 minutes until golden and crispy. Turn them over and seal the other side for a couple of minutes. Transfer to a plate.

In the same pan, add the onion, red pepper, chilli and bay leaves. Cook gently for 5 minutes to soften the onion and pepper. Add the chorizo slices, garlic and half the sliced squid. Continue to cook gently for 5 minutes to release the paprika oils from the chorizo.

Stir in the saffron and smoked paprika and cook for a couple more minutes, then add the tomatoes, giving things a good mix. Add the rice to the pan followed by the stock, lemon juice and some salt and black pepper. Stir well to evenly distribute all the flavours. Now push the pieces of chicken, skin-side up, into the rice and liquid so that the thighs touch the base of the pan and are covered for the most part by liquid. Cook gently, on a wide flame on the hob, without stirring, for 20 minutes.

At the end of this time you may need to add a little more liquid if you think the paella is getting too dry and the rice is still far from being cooked (tip the pan a little so you can see how much water is under the surface). If you do need more liquid, simply pour a little boiling water or hot stock over the surface of the rice: don't stir it in, just let the liquid naturally find its way through the grains.

Now push the mussels, prawns and remaining squid into the bed of rice in the pan and continue to cook for a further 10 minutes until the rice is tender and plump and the seafood cooked. Discard any mussel shells that have not opened. A couple of minutes before it is ready, sprinkle over the cooked runner beans.

Turn off the heat. Arrange lemon wedges all over the paella and sprinkle it with chopped parsley. Cover with a damp tea towel for 5 minutes before serving. This absorbs any remaining moisture and gives you the time to get everyone to the table and prepare them for the unveiling of your beautiful dish!

CHICKEN CACCIATORE

Several people have told me that I should include a chicken cacciatore in this book (page 84). The key to this dish is to use bright red ripe cherry tomatoes that will make the sauce incredibly fruity.

For a dish with relatively few ingredients, this one really packs a punch of flavour.

Serves 4

8 chicken thighs (about 1kg), skin on
salt and freshly ground black pepper
4 tbsp extra virgin olive oil
10 garlic cloves, unpeeled
2 bay leaves
1 onion, finely chopped

250ml white wine
900g cherry tomatoes, halved

To serve:
torn fresh basil leaves

Season the chicken thighs with salt and black pepper. Heat the oil in a wide pan that has a lid and will fit the chicken thighs in one layer, then add the chicken thighs, skin-side down, along with the garlic cloves and bay leaves. Cook on a moderate heat for 5–7 minutes until the chicken skin is golden and crispy, then turn over and seal the second side for a minute or so. Transfer to a plate. You may need to fry the chicken in batches.

Remove the garlic cloves from the pan and set aside for later. Tip the onion into the pan that was used to fry the chicken and cook it for 7–10 minutes on a moderate heat until soft.

Add the wine, increase the heat and boil to reduce by about a half, then add the halved tomatoes. At this point squish out the garlic from their skins and plop them into the pan. The garlic should be soft and pulpy so it will break down into the sauce as it cooks. Season with salt and black pepper and allow the tomatoes to cook for about 15 minutes on a moderate heat until they have turned pulpy and started to thicken a little.

Add the chicken pieces to the tomatoes, pushing them down into the sauce. Cook on a moderate heat for another 30 minutes until the chicken is ready and the sauce has become rich, thick and fruity with reduced tomato juices.

During cooking, give the pan regular shakes and scrapes to ensure nothing is sticking to the bottom. Also, it's a good idea to turn the chicken thighs over halfway through to make sure they cook evenly.

Serve sprinkled with some torn basil leaves.

DUCK BRAISED IN RED WINE
with raspberries

Red wine and raspberries perfectly complement the richness of the slowly braised duck legs in this recipe.

Serves 4

4 duck legs
(about 200g each), thighs attached
salt and freshly ground black pepper
1 onion, roughly sliced
4 garlic cloves, halved

1 bay leaf
3 sprigs of thyme
200ml red wine
150ml chicken stock
100g raspberries, reserve 12 to serve

Preheat the oven to 160°C/325°F/Fan 150°C/gas mark 3. Trim the duck legs of any excess skin or fat and score the surface of the skin with a sharp knife, taking care not to pierce the flesh, only the skin. Scoring helps the fat to be released and encourages browning.

Season the duck with salt and black pepper and in a dry non-stick frying pan brown the pieces of duck on a medium heat, skin-side down – remember not to crowd the pan, so do this in batches if you have to. The duck will release a lot of fat; drain it as you go (keep it in the fridge for delicious roast potatoes!) and continue browning for about 7 minutes until most of the fat has rendered and the skin side is a deep golden brown colour. Quickly seal the other side for a couple of minutes and set aside on a plate.

In the same pan, heat a little of the melted duck fat and gently soften the onion for about 10 minutes. Add the garlic, bay leaf and thyme and continue to cook for a further 2 minutes. Pour in the wine and stock and add some salt and black pepper, scraping the base of the pan to release any tasty morsels stuck to the base. Bring to the boil, then add the raspberries. Pour this into a casserole dish that has a lid and is big enough to hold the duck legs in one layer, then rest the duck legs, skin-side up, on top of the onion and wine mixture. Cover with the lid and pop in the oven for 1½ hours, by which time the duck will be meltingly tender.

Remove the duck from the juices in the pan and keep warm whilst you finish the dish. Push the braising mixture through a sieve using the back of a wooden spoon – try to push as much of the juices through as possible – then pour the sieved juices into the braising pan and boil rapidly on the hob for about 5 minutes until the sauce has reduced to the thickness of single cream. Add some salt and black pepper if you think it needs it, and stir in the reserved fresh raspberries.

Serve the sauce in a jug alongside the duck legs with some creamy mash or sautéed potatoes.

LAMB WITH TOMATOES, OLIVES AND ANCHOVIES

Anchovies go incredibly well with lamb. Build on this with some lemon, olives and tomatoes and you've got the zesty Mediterranean saltiness that I love. Cook this dish (page 70, bottom) and you'll know what I mean!

Serves 4

3 tbsp olive oil
900g lamb shoulder, trimmed of excess fat and cut into 3–4cm pieces
2 onions, roughly chopped
30g tinned anchovies, roughly chopped
2 garlic cloves, thinly sliced
2 glasses of white wine (about 350ml)
2 sprigs of thyme
2 bay leaves
2 pinches of dried oregano
400g tin chopped tomatoes
80g green olives, stones removed

(you can use black olives, but if so, use ones with the stone in; often stoneless black olives are just dyed green olives)
juice and grated zest of 1 lemon
1 red pepper, deseeded and cut into 1cm slices
salt and freshly ground black pepper

To serve:
grated Parmesan
chopped fresh parsley

Preheat the oven to 160°C/325°F/Fan 150°C/gas mark 3. Heat the oil in a heavy based, flameproof casserole dish that has a lid and brown the lamb pieces for 3–4 minutes until well coloured on all sides. You may need to do this in batches. Once browned, transfer the meat to a bowl and set aside.

Add the onions to the hot oil, adding a splash more oil and a little water if too dry, and fry gently for 7–10 minutes until soft and translucent. Add the anchovies and garlic and continue to cook for another couple of minutes until the anchovies have started to break down.

Add the wine, thyme, bay leaves and oregano to the pan and bring to the boil. Then throw in the tomatoes, olives, lemon zest and juice as well as a few grinds of black pepper and a couple of pinches of salt. Now return the browned lamb and any accumulated meat juices to the pan along with the red peppers. Cover with a lid and cook in the oven for 2 hours.

Remove the lid and cook for up to a further 30 minutes until the sauce has reduced and you're left with a rich stew and tender lamb.

Serve topped with grated Parmesan and a little chopped parsley.

MARINATED ZESTY LAMB SALAD
with pine nuts and raisins

This is a delicious way of using slow-cooked lamb. It's quite a rich meat so the lemon works really well to balance the dish, and the mint and parsley added just before serving give it a wonderful freshness.

Serves 4

For cooking the lamb:
1.5kg lamb shoulder on the bone,
cut into 3 pieces (ask your butcher to do this)
¼ tsp sweet smoked paprika
¼ tsp salt
juice of 1 lemon
1 tbsp extra virgin olive oil
2 garlic cloves, bruised

For the salad:
6 tbsp extra virgin olive oil
3 bay leaves
pinch of ground cloves
pinch of cayenne pepper
grated zest of 1 lemon
60g pine nuts
juice of 2–3 lemons
4 tbsp raisins
1 tsp sugar
1 tbsp balsamic vinegar
salt and freshly ground black pepper

To serve:
3 tbsp roughly chopped fresh parsley
3 tbsp roughly chopped fresh mint

Preheat the oven to 150°C/300°F/Fan 140°C/gas mark 2. Trim the lamb of any excess fat. Mix the smoked paprika, salt, lemon juice, olive oil and garlic in a bowl. Rub this mixture into the lamb pieces and pack them tightly into a heavy casserole dish that has a lid. Pour over any of the oil mixture that might be left in the bowl, cover with the lid and cook in the oven for 2½ hours.

Meanwhile, prepare the salad ingredients. In a bowl, mix the olive oil, bay leaves, ground cloves, cayenne pepper and lemon zest. Heat a dry frying pan on the hob until hot and throw in the pine nuts. On a gentle heat, allow them to toast for about 3 minutes until golden – don't take your eyes off them as they can burn really easily. When golden, immediately tip the pine nuts into the oil mixture and stir around. This will warm the oil and encourage the flavours from the spices and bay leaves to be released. Set aside for 30 minutes.

Add the juice from 2 of the lemons, the raisins, sugar, balsamic vinegar and a few good pinches of salt and grinds of black pepper to the infusing salad ingredients. Mix everything to ensure all the flavours are well incorporated.

After 2½ hours the lamb should be meltingly soft and falling off the bone. Remove the pieces from the pot and allow to cool a little on a plate. Now, using your hands, pull the pieces of meat apart into mouthful-sized strips, discarding any bone, fat or gristle as you go. Drop the warm pieces straight into the salad ingredients and mix them to distribute all the flavours evenly. Lastly, stir through the freshly chopped herbs, and, if you think it needs it, add the juice of the third lemon. Serve the marinated lamb alongside a crisp green salad with hunks of bread.

Tip – This dish doesn't like being put into the fridge so it's best eaten no more than 30 minutes after it has been prepared.

It's also delicious made with leftover roast chicken instead of the lamb.

SLOW-ROAST LAMB SHOULDER
with red wine, garlic, rosemary and haricot beans

I first made this pot-roast shoulder of lamb when I was a private chef in France. It was my first day on the job so I wanted to impress with great food throughout the day. Having already cooked a pretty hefty lunch, though, this probably was not the wisest choice for dinner. In fact, I think the whole family had to go straight to bed after the meal to aid digestion of the day's pickings! It was salad from then on ...

Slow-roasting a lamb shoulder works fantastically well since it makes the meat exceptionally tender and generates a delicious sauce all on its own while you sit back and relax.

Serves 6

1.5kg rolled shoulder of lamb
(ask your butcher to trim off as much fat as possible)
salt and freshly ground black pepper
1 tbsp olive oil
2 onions, roughly chopped
6 garlic cloves, peeled and bruised

(whack them with the base of your hand)
1 large sprig of fresh thyme
1 large sprig of fresh rosemary
500ml red wine
400g tin chopped tomatoes
500g cooked haricot beans
(about 2 tins), rinsed and drained

Preheat the oven to 160°C/325°F/Fan 150°C/gas mark 3. Season the lamb with salt and black pepper. Heat the oil in a heavy based, flameproof casserole dish that has a lid and will hold the lamb. When the oil is hot, brown the joint all over, melting any remaining fat on the outside of the meat. This takes about 10 minutes. Once the lamb is nicely coloured, remove and set aside. Check to see how much melted fat you have; you need about 3 tablespoons for the next bit. If there's a lot more, pour some of it away. If there's not enough, add a little more olive oil.

Add the onions to the dish and cook, on a low heat, for 10 minutes until soft and transparent. Then add the garlic, thyme and rosemary and cook for another couple of minutes before adding the red wine, tomatoes and some salt and black pepper. Bring to simmering point, then return the lamb to the dish. Pop the dish, with the lid on, into the oven for 2 hours, giving it a shake and a baste from time to time. Remove, add the beans and replace the lid. Return to the oven for 30 minutes more until the beans have warmed through and the sauce thickened.

Check the sauce for seasoning, then serve the beans and rich sauce under a couple of hunks of meltingly soft lamb. This dish doesn't really need anything else except a green salad and some good wine.

Note - This is equally good with lamb shanks, but you may need a bigger pot.

LAMB STEW
with lemon, potatoes and feta

Lamb goes beautifully with the lemon and potatoes in this light summery stew. This one comes, with thanks, from my business partner, Mark, who's been cooking it for years after getting it from a friend who got it off a friend, off a friend, off a friend ... I've changed Mark's recipe a little. He chops half a whole lemon and puts this into the recipe; I use the zest from two lemons and then the flesh from half a lemon, removing the bitter pith before chopping up and adding to the stew. If you try both ways, Mark and I would be happy to hear which you prefer!

Serves 4–6

3 tbsp olive oil
900g trimmed lamb shoulder,
diced into 3–4cm pieces
2 onions, roughly chopped
2 lemons
2 garlic cloves, finely chopped
400g fresh ripe tomatoes,
roughly chopped
1 tbsp fresh oregano leaves
or 1 tsp of dried
2–3 sprigs of fresh thyme
375ml vegetable stock
salt and freshly ground black pepper
500g waxy potatoes,
peeled and cut into 2–3cm cubes

To serve:
175g feta cheese
4 tbsp roughly chopped fresh parsley

Preheat the oven to 160°C/325°F/Fan 150°C/gas mark 3. Heat the oil in a heavy based, flameproof casserole dish that has a lid and brown the lamb in 2 or 3 batches until nicely coloured on all sides. This will take 3–4 minutes per batch. Transfer the browned lamb to a bowl and keep warm.

Throw the onions into the pan and cook gently for 10–12 minutes until softened and turning golden at the edges. Add a little more oil and a splash of water if the pan seems to be drying out and scrape off any stuck-on bits at the bottom of the pan.

Meanwhile, grate the zest from both the lemons. Be careful not to grate any of the white pith, as this will give a nasty bitter edge to your stew. Cut the top and bottom off one of the lemons to create flat ends. Using a knife, cut down the sides of the lemon, following its natural contours and remove all the white pith. Now cut half of the 'pithless' lemon into small pieces, discarding any pips you find along the way.

Once the onions have softened and are starting to turn brown, add the garlic and cook for a couple more minutes. Add the tomatoes, lemon zest and the chopped lemon flesh, oregano, thyme and vegetable stock. Stir through a few pinches of salt and grinds of black pepper before returning the browned lamb to the pot along with any collected juices. Bring to simmering point and reduce the heat so it bubbles gently. Cover with the lid slightly at a slant to let some steam escape, then pop the dish into the oven for 1 hour.

Add the potatoes to the stew and cook for a further hour until the potatoes and lamb are completely tender and the sauce thickened. Just before serving, either stir the feta into the stew, allowing it to melt for a few minutes, or simply sprinkle it over the top with a scattering of chopped parsley.

KLEFTIKO
Slow-baked shoulder of lamb with lemon, garlic and oregano

Kleftiko literally means 'stolen meat' and owes its name to shady goings-on in the Greek countryside. Bandits who didn't own their flocks would steal sheep and cook the stolen meat in underground clay pits to prevent any smoke being seen and thereby avoiding being caught. It's easier to get your lamb from the butcher or the supermarket!

The dish is so simple yet absolutely delicious. The meat falls from the bone with a tap of a spoon and the juices left in the pan are impossibly good. It's really important to seal your pot as tightly as possible to keep all the moisture from evaporating away.

Serves 5–6

1.5kg lamb shoulder, bone in, cut into 5–6 pieces
(get your butcher to do this)
8 garlic cloves, halved
grated zest and juice of 3 lemons
3 tbsp extra virgin olive oil
salt and freshly ground black pepper
1 tbsp dried oregano or a few sprigs of fresh
3–4 potatoes (about 500g), peeled and halved
(try to use waxy ones like Cyprus potatoes)
2 onions, peeled and quartered

Preheat the oven to 150°C/300°F/Fan 140°C/gas mark 2. Trim the pieces of lamb of as much fat as possible, reserving a couple of small pieces of fat. Heat a large, heavy based, flameproof casserole dish that has a lid and melt the reserved fat on a medium heat for 2–3 minutes. Place the lamb pieces, a couple at a time, fat-/skin-side down in the pan and brown them for 3–5 minutes until coloured and the fat has mostly melted. Remove and set aside in a bowl or on a plate and do the same with the remaining pieces. Pour away any fat accumulated in the pan.

With a knife, make 2 or 3 holes in the flesh of each piece of lamb and stuff with some garlic.

In a large bowl, combine the lemon zest and juice, olive oil, some black pepper, a few generous pinches of salt and the oregano. If you're using fresh oregano leaves, crush them a bit in your hands before adding to help release their flavour. Then rub this all over the lamb pieces, potatoes and onions.

Pour the whole lot back into the casserole dish used for browning the lamb. Scrunch up a large piece of baking parchment and push it onto the lamb, potato and onion mixture, tucking the sides around the edges of the ingredients. Then cover the pan with tin foil as tightly as you can, secure with the lid, and pop in the oven for 3½ hours. Don't be tempted to have a peek during the cooking time!

Remove the pot from the oven and carefully lift out the pieces of lamb and the potatoes and onions. Try to skim as much fat as you can from the juices in the pan, or pour the juices into a bowl and store in the fridge overnight, allowing any fat to solidify. Whichever method you have chosen, put the fat-free juices together with the pieces of lamb, potatoes and onions back in a pot and bring up to heat in the oven or on the hob.

Serve with some plain bulgur wheat and a tomato salad. Be sure to mop up all those lemony garlicky juices.

NAVARIN OF LAMB

This French lamb stew is a little bit fiddly but if you make the effort you'll be left with a beautiful, shiny, rich meaty sauce with tender lamb and perfectly 'al dente' veg. Unlike most stews, you make it in stages rather than chucking all the ingredients in a pan at the beginning, so it's not one to throw in the oven before going out to walk the dog. You need to spend time with a navarin of lamb!

Serves 4

2 tbsp olive oil
900g lamb shoulder,
as much fat removed as possible then diced
1 tbsp caster sugar
1 tbsp flour
salt and freshly ground black pepper
150ml white wine
400ml chicken or beef stock
2 bay leaves
2 sprigs of thyme
2 tbsp tomato purée
2 garlic cloves, crushed

To finish the sauce:
lemon juice
25g butter

Vegetables:
12 peeled shallots (submerge the shallots in boiling water for a minute before cooling – the skins are much easier to remove)
2 carrots, peeled and cut into chunks, or 8 baby carrots
2 small turnips (about 300g), peeled and cut into chunks
350g baby new potatoes, peeled or unpeeled
(depending on your preference)
75g petits pois or small garden peas

Preheat your grill to its highest setting and preheat the oven to 150°C/300°F/Fan 140°C/gas mark 2. Heat the oil in a flameproof casserole dish that has a lid, then brown the lamb for 3–5 minutes in batches. Remove each batch to a baking tray big enough to hold all the pieces in a single layer.

Sprinkle the pieces of lamb in the baking tray with the sugar and flour and season with salt and black pepper. Pop under the grill for 5–10 minutes until the sugar and flour have caramelised.

Meanwhile, on a low heat, pour the wine into the casserole dish used to brown the lamb and scrape off any bits from the base. Add the stock, bay leaves, thyme, tomato purée and garlic and a little more salt and black pepper. Turn off the heat.

Once the lamb under the grill has caramelised, add it to the wine and stock mixture in the casserole dish. Use some of the stock and wine mixture to release any juices and stuck-on bits from the baking tray used for the lamb and also add this to the casserole dish. Cover with a lid and put into the oven for 2 hours until the lamb is tender.

Whilst the lamb is cooking, prepare all the vegetables and cook each separately in several pans of boiling water. As soon as each vegetable is cooked, plunge them into cold water to stop them cooking further, then drain and set aside.

When tender, remove the lamb from the sauce and transfer to a plate or bowl. Put the casserole dish on top of the stove, skim off any fat and boil the sauce to reduce it, skimming off any impurities and fat that rise to the surface.

When you've got a rich sauce the consistency of single cream, taste for seasoning. Add a squeeze of lemon juice if you think it needs it, then simply whisk in the butter and return the meat to the sauce along with all the vegetables to heat them through gently for 3–4 minutes.

Serve!

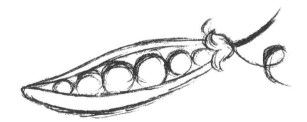

BEEF CARBONNADE

The dark beer, sugar and vinegar in this Belgian classic give it a wonderfully rich colour and taste. It's traditionally eaten with crusty croutons topped with tangy mustard, giving a great mix of flavours and textures.

Serves 4

2 tbsp olive oil
salt and freshly ground black pepper
900g beef chuck steak, cut into 3–4cm pieces
100g unsmoked lardons or bacon pieces
4 medium onions, finely sliced
1 tbsp soft brown muscovado sugar
2 garlic cloves, finely chopped

1 tbsp plain flour
500ml dark Belgian beer (Leffe Brune, for example)
3 tbsp red wine vinegar
1 bay leaf
2 sprigs of fresh thyme
Dijon or wholegrain mustard
4 thick slices of a French stick

Preheat the oven to 160°C/325°F/Fan 150°C/gas mark 3. Heat the oil in a heavy based, flameproof casserole dish that has a lid. Grind some black pepper over the pieces of beef, then brown them for about 3–4 minutes, in batches, in the hot oil. When each batch is done, transfer to a bowl and keep warm.

When you've browned all the meat, add the lardons or bacon pieces to the dish and cook for a couple of minutes until the fat has melted. Add the onions and cook slowly for 20 minutes until they are nice and soft and starting to turn golden. Next, add the sugar and garlic and continue to cook for another 5 minutes until the onions are starting to caramelise.

Add the flour and cook for a couple of minutes, then pour in the beer. Make sure you scrape off any bits from the bottom of the pan and dissolve them into the beery liquor. Add the vinegar, bay leaf, thyme sprigs and a couple of generous pinches of salt to the dish along with the browned beef with any of its collected juices. Bring to simmering point, then cover with the lid and pop into the oven for 1½–2 hours until the sauce has reduced and become quite thick and the beef is tender.

Remove the casserole dish from the oven and test for seasoning. To finish it off, spread a thin layer of mustard on each of the slices of bread and place them, mustard-side up, on top of the stew. Raise the oven temperature to 190°C/375°F/Fan 180°C/gas mark 5 and put the pot, uncovered, back in the oven for 30 minutes or until the croutons have browned.

Serve from the pot alongside a bowl of crushed new potatoes with horseradish and let everyone help themselves.

BEEF BRAISED IN BAROLO

Barolo is quite a pricey wine, so use a Barbaresco if you like; it will be kinder on your pocket but is equally full bodied. Start preparing this dish the night before you want to serve it so the meat has had a good time to marinate before cooking.

Serves 6

For the marinade:
1 bottle Barolo or
Barbaresco red wine
2 bay leaves
4 sage leaves
1 sprig of rosemary
10 peppercorns

For the dish:
4 tbsp olive oil
1.5kg rolled topside or silverside of beef
salt and freshly ground black pepper
1 **onion**, roughly chopped
2 **carrots**, peeled and roughly chopped
2 **celery sticks**, roughly chopped

Mix together all the marinade ingredients and put in a large non-metallic bowl with the beef, rolling it to coat. Set aside in the fridge for 12–24 hours, turning the meat a couple of times along the way. Remove the beef from the marinade and dry it well with kitchen paper. Reserve the marinade for later.

Preheat the oven to 150°C/300°F/Fan 140°C/gas mark 2. Heat the oil in a flameproof casserole dish which has a lid and will snugly fit the beef. Season the beef with salt and black pepper and brown for 2–3 minutes on all sides before transferring the meat to a plate. Add the onion, carrots and celery to the pan and cook on a moderate heat for about 10 minutes until the onion has softened and is starting to brown at the edges.

Pop the meat back in the dish along with the reserved marinade. Cover with the lid and cook in the oven for 3 hours, turning the beef over halfway through.

Remove the beef from the dish and transfer to a serving dish, covering it with tin foil to keep warm. Skim off any excess fat from the sauce and vegetables in the dish. Discard the rosemary sprig and bay leaves and, using a hand blender, blend the sauce and vegetables to a pulp, then push it through a sieve using the back of a wooden spoon. You want to end up with a thick sauce, so you may need to reduce it on a high heat in the pan for 5–10 minutes. Taste for seasoning and serve the sauce over slices of the carved beef.

BEEF STIFADO

This is an aromatic sweet-and-sour stew from Greece.

Serves 4

For the marinade:
350ml red wine
5 cloves
1 cinnamon stick, broken in two
4 garlic cloves, thinly sliced
2 bay leaves
1 tsp dried oregano
6 allspice berries
4 tbsp red wine vinegar
grated zest and juice of ½ orange

For the stew:
900g beef chuck steak, cut into 5–7cm pieces
3 tbsp olive oil
1 onion, roughly chopped
2 celery sticks, roughly chopped
1 carrot, peeled and roughly chopped
16 shallots, peeled and left whole
(submerge in a bowl of boiling water for 1 minute and then
plunge into cold water. The skins will slip off easily.)
400g tin chopped tomatoes
1 tbsp tomato purée
1½ tbsp sugar
30g currants
salt and freshly ground black pepper

To serve:
chopped fresh parsley

Mix together all the ingredients for the marinade, then pour it over the beef in a non-metallic bowl, stirring to coat all the pieces. Cover and leave overnight in the fridge to marinate.

The following day, preheat the oven to 160°C/325°F/Fan 150°C/gas mark 3. Remove the meat from the marinade, shaking off as much liquid as you can, and dry the pieces with some kitchen paper – try to get the pieces as dry as possible otherwise they will spatter in the fat. Reserve the marinade for later.

In a heavy based, flameproof casserole dish that has a lid, heat the olive oil and brown the meat for 3–4 minutes (in batches if necessary) before setting aside in a bowl. Add the onion, celery, carrot and shallots to the pan and cook gently until the onion is soft. Add a little more oil and a splash of water if the pan is too dry.

Pour in the reserved marinade followed by the tomatoes, tomato purée, sugar, currants and the browned meat. Finish with a few grinds of black pepper and some generous pinches of salt. Make sure everything is well combined.

Put the lid on the pan and cook in the oven for 2–2½ hours until the sauce has thickened and the beef is tender. Serve scattered with chopped parsley and accompanied by pasta or rice.

SLOW-COOKED BEEF STROGANOFF

Beef stroganoff is traditionally made with fillet of beef and is quite tricky to make. This version, however, is a slow-cook method that makes life much easier and cheaper!

Serves 4

50g butter
2 tbsp olive oil
800g chuck steak,
cut into 1cm thick strips
1 onion, thinly sliced
75ml brandy
2 tbsp tomato purée
250ml white wine
100ml beef stock

salt and freshly ground black pepper
300g button mushrooms, halved
4–6 tbsp soured cream

To serve:
4–6 tsp soured cream
sweet paprika
chopped fresh parsley

Preheat the oven to 160°C/325°F/Fan 150°C/gas mark 3, or you can cook this on the hob. Melt half the butter with the oil in a heavy based, flameproof casserole dish that has a lid. When the fat is hot, add the pieces of beef and fry to seal for 2–3 minutes; you want a little colour on the beef, so you'll probably need to do this in batches. As each batch is ready, set it aside in a bowl for later.

Once all the beef has browned and is eagerly waiting in a bowl, add the remaining butter to the pan. Tip in the onion and cook slowly on a low heat for 12–15 minutes until it is very soft but not colouring.

Add the brandy to the pan and cook on a high heat for a minute or so to drive off all the alcohol. Then add the tomato purée and continue to cook for another minute. Pour in the wine and beef stock, some salt and black pepper. Bring to the boil before returning the browned meat, with any juices, back to the pan along with the button mushrooms. Cover with the lid and cook in the oven or on a low heat on the hob for 1½–2 hours until the beef is tender and the sauce thickened.

Just before serving, stir in 4–6 teaspoons of soured cream (depending on your personal taste) and check for seasoning.

Serve with some rice and top each portion of stroganoff with another teaspoon of soured cream, a dusting of paprika and a sprinkling of chopped parsley.

BOEUF BOURGUIGNON

No introduction is needed for this classic French beef stew made with red wine, caramelised whole shallots and mushrooms.

Serves 4

salt and freshly ground black pepper
900g beef chuck steak, cut into 3–4cm pieces
3 tbsp olive oil
100g unsmoked lardons or bacon pieces
1 onion, roughly chopped
2 garlic cloves, finely chopped
1 tbsp plain flour
600ml red wine (ideally a nice Burgundy)

1 bouquet garni (1 stick celery, 1 bay leaf, a sprig of fresh thyme and a couple of parsley stalks tied with string)
16 shallots
30g butter
150g button or chestnut mushrooms

To serve:
2 tbsp chopped fresh parsley

Preheat the oven to 160°C/325°F/Fan 150°C/gas mark 3. Grind some black pepper over the beef. Heat the oil in a heavy based, flameproof casserole dish that has a lid, then brown the beef in batches for 3–4 minutes or until caramelised on all sides. Set aside the cooked meat in a bowl.

Add the lardons or bacon pieces to the pan, cooking for a couple of minutes until the fat has melted and the pieces have started to brown. Then tip in the onion and garlic and gently cook for about 10 minutes until the onion is soft. Add the flour to the pan, stirring well to combine and cook on a low heat for a couple of minutes before pouring in the wine. Turn up the heat and reduce the liquid by about 50 per cent. Add the bouquet garni and a couple of good pinches of salt and return the browned beef and juices to the dish. Cover with the lid, place in the oven and cook for 1½ hours.

Whilst the stew is cooking, remove the skins from the shallots by plunging them into some boiling water for a minute. Drain, and let them cool a little before removing the end of the root with a knife and slipping the skins off. Melt half the butter in a frying pan and cook the whole shallots for 10–15 minutes on a low heat until caramelised. Remove to a bowl and set aside. Melt the remaining butter in the frying pan and cook the whole mushrooms for about 10 minutes until browned. Add the mushrooms to the bowl with the shallots.

Once the stew has been cooking for 1½ hours, add the caramelised onions and mushrooms, stir to combine then pop it back in the oven for another 30 minutes until the beef is completely tender and the sauce has thickened. Feel free to remove the lid if you want a thicker stew.

Remove the bouquet garni, check for seasoning and serve with the parsley scattered over the top. Great with some simple mashed spuds!

OSSO BUCO

Veal shin gives an incredibly rich and velvety dimension to the sauce in this fantastic Italian dish. Traditionally served with risotto Milanese (risotto flavoured with saffron), I think this is equally good simply with some creamy mashed potato or Parmesan polenta (see page 154).

Serves 4

3 tbsp extra virgin olive oil
4 pieces of shin of veal, cut 3–4cm thick
salt and freshly ground black pepper
2 onions, roughly chopped
2 carrots, roughly chopped
2 celery sticks, roughly chopped
3 garlic cloves, thinly sliced
2 bay leaves

2 glasses of white wine (about 350ml)
150ml chicken stock
400g tin chopped tomatoes

For the gremolata:
grated zest of 1 lemon
1 garlic clove, finely chopped
2 tbsp chopped fresh parsley

Heat the oil in a flameproof casserole dish that has a lid and is big enough to fit all 4 pieces of meat in one layer. Season the veal pieces with salt and black pepper, then brown each side in the hot oil for 2–3 minutes. Transfer to a plate and keep warm.

Using the same pan, throw in the onions, carrots, celery and garlic along with the bay leaves. If it's feeling a bit dry, add a splash more oil and a little water. Cook gently for about 15 minutes until the onions have softened and turned translucent. Add the wine, stock, tomatoes and some salt and black pepper to the pan. When it's all bubbling, return the veal shins to the pan.

Scrunch up a large piece of greaseproof paper, unscrunch it and then push it directly on top of the veal, tucking it around the edges of the meat along the sides of the dish – this will prevent the liquid from evaporating too much. Cover with a lid and cook gently for 2–2½ hours until the meat begins to fall off the bone.

At this point, gently remove the meat from the sauce, transfer to a plate and keep warm. Put the dish on the hob, turn up the heat and reduce the sauce until it has thickened slightly.

Meanwhile, prepare the gremolata by mixing together the lemon zest, garlic and chopped parsley in a bowl.

Serve the reduced sauce spooned over the cooked meat and sprinkle with the gremolata.

POT AU FEU

Every family in France must have their own version of this celebrated, easy, yet delicious dish. Some insist on a mix of meats, including pork (cured and uncured), lamb, beef and chicken; others keep it simple with just a piece of beef, which is what I have chosen for this recipe.

The trick to a good *pot au feu* lies in the initial skimming and gentle cooking, where bubbles only just rise to the surface. This will give you a perfectly clear broth and tender meat.

Serves 6

1.5 kg rolled silverside or topside of beef, or 6 slices of shin of beef (bone in) cut into 4cm thick slices – or a mixture!
500g veal bones (ideally shin)
5 litres water
2 onions, unpeeled and quartered
3 garlic cloves, peeled and halved
2 cloves
3 sprigs of fresh thyme
2 bay leaves

10 peppercorns
1 tbsp salt
2 carrots, peeled and cut into large chunks
3 celery sticks, cut into large chunks
2 leeks, cleaned and cut into large chunks
1 fennel bulb, cut lengthways into 6

To serve:
Dijon mustard
cornichons

Pop the beef joint or shin along with the veal bones into a deep pan that has a lid. Pour the water over and slowly bring the liquid to simmering point. As the temperature increases, scum and impurities will rise to the surface, so skim these off with a large spoon and discard. Once simmering point has been reached, turn the heat down so only a few bubbles reach the surface. This is very important as it will help you make a really clear broth. Continue skimming for another 15 minutes or until no more impurities rise to the surface.

Drop the onions, garlic, cloves, thyme, bay leaves, peppercorns and salt into the broth. Place the lid on a slant on top of the pot to allow steam to escape, then cook very gently for 3 hours. All the while you want only a few bubbles rising to the surface; any more, and it's cooking too fast. After 3 hours, skim off any excess fat, then drop in the carrots, celery, leeks and fennel and cook for a further 30 minutes – again, very gently.

Remove the meat from the broth and discard the onion skins. Let the meat rest for a few minutes while you test the seasoning of the broth. Add some more salt if you think it needs it.

Slice the beef (or serve up a piece of beef shin) and plate it up with the vegetables in bowls with some of the broth. Serve with Dijon mustard and cornichons, the traditional accompaniments to pot au feu.

HUNGARIAN GOULASH

Perhaps rather like chilli con carne, Hungarian goulash has lost its way. This version, however, spiced with sweet Hungarian paprika and caraway seeds, is a real treat. Make sure you use Hungarian paprika as it really makes a world of difference to the flavour.

In Hungary, goulash is traditionally more of a soup than a stew. So, if you want to turn this recipe into a stew, simply add more water with perhaps a few chopped potatoes towards the end of the cooking time to thicken the liquor.

Serves 4

2 tbsp olive oil
2 onions, roughly chopped
900g chuck steak, trimmed of as much fat as possible and cut into 3–4cm pieces
2 garlic cloves, roughly chopped
1 tsp caraway seeds
2½ tbsp Hungarian sweet paprika
390g tin chopped tomatoes
450ml water
salt and freshly ground black pepper
1 red pepper, cut into 1cm strips
juice of ½ lemon

Heat the oil in a large, heavy based saucepan that has a lid, and gently cook the onions for 5–10 minutes until soft. Turn up the heat and add the chunks of beef, garlic and caraway seeds and cook for 5 minutes or until the beef pieces are sealed. Remove the pan from the heat and add the paprika, stirring well to incorporate the aromatic spice into the meat.

Return to the heat and add the tomatoes, water, a few pinches of salt and some black pepper. Cook, covered, for 1½ hours on the hob on a low heat. (You could also use your oven if you prefer, heated to 160°C/325°F/Fan 150°C/gas mark 3.)

Add the red pepper and continue to cook, covered, for a further 30 minutes or until the beef is tender and the sauce thickened. Squeeze in the lemon juice and test for seasoning, adding more salt if you think it warrants it.

BLANQUETTE DE VEAU

In the late 90s I taught English in France for a year in the Dordogne. It was a great culinary experience and I was lucky enough to live with Nicole and her son Pierre, who welcomed me into their home with open arms. During my stay, I managed to astound them that an English lad could cook, and in return Nicole introduced me to some classic French dishes. One dish that I remember well, mainly because I hadn't heard of it at the time, was a slow-cooked veal stew with a creamy white sauce made from the cooking liquor and infused with aromatic herbs and spices. I've recently quizzed Nicole for her recipe and this is it, with a couple of changes here and there.

Do your best to buy British veal, as you can be assured that the animals were kept well.

Serves 4

900g British veal, cut into 3–4cm pieces
1 litre water
1 slice of lemon
175ml white wine
¼ tsp black peppercorns
4 cloves
4 bay leaves
3 sprigs of fresh thyme
1 carrot, peeled and cut into ½cm thick slices
1 celery stick, broken in half
salt and freshly ground black pepper
12 small shallots
30g butter
30g plain flour
2 egg yolks
150ml double cream

To serve:
chopped fresh parsley

Put the veal in a heavy based, flameproof casserole dish that has a lid. Pour over the water (it should cover the veal) and add the slice of lemon. Bring to simmering point on a moderate heat and skim off any scum that rises to the top. Continue to simmer very gently, skimming for 5–10 minutes until the cooking liquor is clear and no more scum or froth rises to the surface.

Add the wine, peppercorns, cloves, bay leaves, thyme, carrot, celery and a couple of pinches of salt to the pot. Simmer very gently for 45 minutes with the lid on at a slant to allow some steam to escape.

Meanwhile, remove the skins from the shallots. To do this, simply plop them into a bowl of boiling water for 30 seconds, then rinse them in cold water to cool them down. You'll easily be able to slip the skins off after you've cut the base of the root and tips off.

Once the stew has been bubbling gently for 45 minutes, add the peeled shallots and continue to cook for a further 15 minutes until the veal is tender.

With a slotted spoon, remove the pieces of meat and the vegetables from the pot, fishing out and discarding the celery and the peppercorns and cloves that you find along the way. Keep the meat and vegetables in a bowl covered with foil to keep warm while you finish the sauce.

Strain the cooking liquor into a bowl. In the heavy based pan, now melt the butter on a low heat before adding the flour. Stir around to mix all the flour into the butter. Once the flour is fully incorporated, add a ladleful at a time of the cooking liquor, using a whisk to prevent any lumps forming and only adding another ladleful once the previous one has been completely mixed in and the sauce returns to its smooth consistency. Once all the liquid has been added, bring it up to simmering point. Allow it to bubble for a couple of minutes to cook the flour thoroughly and keep stirring regularly to avoid any sneaky lumps forming.

In a bowl, mix the egg yolks into the cream. Take the pan of bubbling thickened stock off the heat and, once it has stopped bubbling, pour the cream and egg mixture into it, stirring with a wooden spoon. This will further thicken the sauce a little – you're looking for a consistency similar to single cream. Taste for seasoning and add some salt and black pepper if you think it needs it (which it probably will).

Now tip the reserved meat and vegetables into the white sauce and warm through. Be sure not to boil the sauce as this would result in the egg yolks scrambling, which of course you don't want.

Sprinkle with chopped parsley and serve with plain rice or crusty bread.

MUSHROOM STEW
with thyme and feta

This is a beautifully rich, earthy vegetarian stew (page 70) packed with tasty mushrooms.

Serves 4–6

45g dried porcini mushrooms,
soaked in 250ml boiling water
50g butter
2 onions, thinly sliced
3 garlic cloves, finely sliced
175g shitake mushrooms,
trimmed and halved
300g chestnut mushrooms,
trimmed and halved
180g oyster mushrooms,
torn into chunks

4 sprigs of fresh thyme
2 bay leaves
2 tbsp brandy, Marsala or port
(this dish is quite versatile!)
250ml red wine
1 tbsp tomato purée
salt and freshly ground black pepper

To serve:
chopped fresh parsley
150g feta cheese

Begin by soaking the porcini in the boiling water in a bowl for about 20 minutes.

Melt the butter in a deep saucepan that has a lid, add the onions and cook on a low heat for about 20 minutes. You don't want to colour them, only soften them and drive off the moisture gently, which sweetens the onions beautifully.

Add the garlic and cook for a couple more minutes before throwing in your prepared shitake, chestnut and oyster mushrooms, thyme and bay leaves. The mushrooms will soak up a lot of the fat and juices at first, but don't worry; they will soon let out their own rich juices to moisten the pan again. Cook gently for 10 minutes.

Drain the porcini mushrooms, reserving the soaking liquid, then rinse them under cold water to remove any grit. Once rinsed, add the mushrooms to the cooking stew, give it a good stir and leave to cook gently for 5 more minutes. Line a sieve with some kitchen paper and pour the porcini soaking liquid through to catch any gritty bits. Reserve the strained liquid.

Pour the brandy, Marsala or port into the cooking mushrooms and allow the alcohol to evaporate for a couple of minutes. Add the wine and strained porcini soaking liquid, tomato purée and a few generous pinches of salt and some black pepper. Cover with a lid and cook gently for 20 minutes until the liquid has reduced and you are left with a rich dark stock and soft tasty mushrooms.

Serve sprinkled with some chopped parsley and crumbled feta cheese.

CAPONATA

This delicious aubergine stew from Sicily is made sweet and sour by the addition of sugar and vinegar. It's equally good eaten cold with crusty bread as it is served hot with some pasta or rice. A great meat-free stew.

Serves 4

120ml extra virgin olive oil
750g aubergine, cut into 1.5cm cubes
1 onion, finely chopped
2 celery sticks, fairly finely chopped
3 garlic cloves, thinly sliced
500g fresh chopped tomatoes or 2 tins chopped tomatoes
2 tsp sugar
100g pitted green olives, rinsed and halved
35g capers, rinsed
2 tbsp currants
3 tbsp pine nuts
5 tbsp red wine vinegar
salt and freshly ground black pepper

To serve:
a few fresh basil leaves

Heat 3 tablespoons of the olive oil in a deep, wide non-stick frying pan. When hot, fry half the aubergines on medium heat for 5–7 minutes until golden brown on all sides. Transfer them to a bowl. Add a further 3 tablespoons of oil to the pan and repeat with the remaining aubergine.

Heat the remaining oil in the pan and add the onion, celery and garlic and cook gently for 10–12 minutes until the onions are soft. Add the tomatoes and sugar and continue to cook for 15 minutes, by which time the tomatoes will have completely broken down.

Throw the remaining ingredients into the pan along with some generous pinches of salt and some black pepper as well as the fried aubergines. Cook gently on the hob for a further 10 minutes.

Top with basil leaves and serve either hot or cold.

SWISS CHEESE FONDUE

The ultimate retro one-pot wonder has to be the cheese fondue. This recipe comes from Cecily, a Swiss friend from the market days. She advises avoiding drinking cold liquids with a fondue as it makes the cheese become too heavy in the belly. Instead, drink lots of red wine or some hot tea! Another bit of adventurous advice from Cecily is to dip your bread into a little kirsch before dipping it into the cheese fondue, for a more alcoholic treat ...

I'm afraid you do need a fondue set for this recipe to work best. The ceramic bowl used to melt the cheese on the hob can then be brought to the table where it sits on a trivet over a flame, which keeps the cheese from turning into a solid lump as it cools.

Serves 4

2 garlic cloves, lightly bruised to release their flavour
400ml dry white wine
300g gruyère cheese, coarsely grated
300g strong Cheddar cheese, coarsely grated
(or Beaufort, Emmental, or other hard cheese of your liking)
2 tsp cornflour
80ml kirsch
freshly ground black pepper

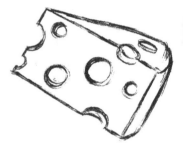

To serve:
1 baguette, cut into 2cm x 2cm cubes (and/or cubes of sourdough bread, carrot batons, radishes, broccoli florets ...)

First prepare all the bread and vegetables for dipping.

Heat the garlic and wine in a fondue pan over a low heat. Once hot, add the cheeses and stir constantly in a figure of eight shape with a wooden spoon until completely melted. The mixture at this stage should be smooth and runny.

Stir the cornflour into the glass of kirsch and add this to the cheese and wine mixture to thicken it. Keep stirring for a few minutes before bringing the pan to the table and resting it on a moderate flame. Grind over some black pepper just before you're about to eat.

As the cheese starts to run out, a nice crust should form at the bottom of the pan. Scrape it off – it's delicious!

ASIA

GREEN CHICKEN CURRY

During a six-week stay in Thailand in 2002 I grew to love Thai food. I was on a diving holiday but it wasn't long before I realised that the meals after dive trips were far more exciting for me than the dives themselves!

This is a classic Thai curry and the recipe is inspired by one of the Australian chef David Thompson's that I first made a couple of years ago. I've taken out a few of the more hard-to-find Thai ingredients to make life easier for you. Fear not – it still tastes fantastic. Making the fresh curry paste really does make a huge difference, creating those intensely fresh flavours characteristic of Thai food. The finished dish looks brilliant too; the rich green of the curry is set off beautifully with fine strips of red chilli, fresh coriander and sweet basil leaves.

Serves 4

For the curry paste:
¼ tsp cumin seeds
¼ tsp coriander seeds
3 tbsp chopped garlic cloves
6 tbsp chopped shallots
pinch of salt
1 tbsp chopped coriander stalks
1 tbsp finely sliced kaffir lime leaves
(use frozen – fresh are almost impossible to find and dried are not the same.
If you can't find either, use the grated zest of fresh limes)
2 tbsp chopped lemongrass
1½ tbsp peeled and chopped galangal (or use ginger)
10 small hot green chillies, chopped (with seeds if you like it fiery)
1 tsp fish sauce

For the curry:
1 tbsp sunflower oil
4 skinless chicken breasts or 8 thigh fillets, cut into chunks
16 pea aubergines (tiny aubergines with a slightly bitter and sour taste,
available from Chinese and Thai supermarkets)
400ml coconut milk
200ml chicken stock
1 tbsp fish sauce
5 shitake mushrooms, quartered
100g baby corn

50g mangetout or sugar snap peas
juice of 1 lime

To serve:
1 long red chilli, deseeded and finely sliced
a handful of coriander leaves
a few Thai basil leaves (or use normal basil)

First make the curry paste – you can use a mortar and pestle if you're feeling strong or a small blender if you're not. Roast the cumin and coriander seeds in a dry pan on the hob for a couple of minutes. Just when they start smoking, transfer them to a mortar and pestle, allow to cool and grind to a powder.

Next, using your hand blender (or continue to use the mortar and pestle if you're up for it), whizz the ground spices with the garlic and shallots, blending to a pulp with the help of a pinch of salt. Then add the coriander stalks, kaffir lime leaves, lemongrass, galangal, chillies and the fish sauce. Blend or grind until you have a homogeneous, aromatic green paste. Feel free to give it a taste but it'll be pretty spicy, so watch out.

Now make the curry (the easy bit). Heat the oil in a wok until smoking, then add 5 tablespoons of the curry paste. Keep it moving and fry for a couple of minutes to release the flavours. Be sure not to burn it. Add the chicken and pea aubergines to the pan, stirring to coat the chicken and seal it. Then add the coconut milk and stock, followed by the fish sauce and mushrooms. Bring to simmering point and cook for 5 minutes, then add the corn and mangetout or sugar snaps and cook for a further 5 minutes until the chicken is cooked and the sauce has thickened a little.

Add the lime juice and taste for seasoning. If it's not salty enough add more fish sauce; add more lime if it's not acidic enough. Ladle into bowls and top with slices of red chilli, coriander leaves and a couple of basil leaves. Serve with steamed rice.

Tip – If you'd rather a meat-free version, replace the chicken in this recipe with pieces of cod, haddock or prawns, but add these only at the end of cooking, just after the mangetout.

AROMATIC THAI CHICKEN STEW
with broccoli and shitake mushrooms

This looks as beautiful as it tastes (page 108).

Serves 4

For the base:
400ml coconut milk
400ml chicken stock
2 lemongrass stalks, broken into pieces
and bruised (bash it with a rolling pin)
5cm piece of fresh ginger
(don't bother to peel it), bruised (as above!)
4 garlic cloves, bruised
5 shallots, roughly chopped
pared zest of 1 lime
(be careful not to use the pith as this will
make the dish bitter)
5 kaffir lime leaves
(or pared zest of another 2 limes)
2 small hot green chillies,
sliced (with seeds)

pinch of ground turmeric
3 tbsp fish sauce
1 tsp sugar

For the stew:
4 chicken breasts or 8 thigh fillets,
sliced into ½ cm strips
85g shitake mushrooms, quartered
100g broccoli florets
or trimmed sprouting broccoli
juice of 1 lime
200g beansprouts

To serve:
fresh coriander leaves
1 thinly sliced red chilli, deseeded

In a saucepan, heat the coconut milk and stock. Once it's hot, add all the other ingredients for the base. Cook on a very low heat for 30 minutes to give all the ingredients time to impart their individual flavours to the coconut milk, then sieve the mixture to leave an aromatic coconut base. Make sure you push through the lumps in the sieve with the back of a spoon to extract as much of their flavour as possible. Make this a couple of hours in advance, if you want.

Add the chicken and shitake mushrooms and cook on a moderate heat for 7–10 minutes. Add the broccoli a couple of minutes before the end of the cooking time and continue to simmer until both the chicken and broccoli are cooked.

Mix in the lime juice and taste. You might need to add more fish sauce if it's not salty enough, more lime if it's not acidic enough, or more sugar if it's too acidic. It's all about the balance!

Pile some beansprouts into bowls followed by ladles of your aromatic stew. Top with fresh coriander leaves and sliced red chilli.

TONJIRU
Japanese pork and miso soup

Tonjiru (page 109, bottom) is absolutely delicious and takes no time at all to make. This recipe comes from Emma and Ken who run Tsuru, a fantastic Japanese sushi bar in London. Their sushi and sashimi are amongst the freshest and most beautifully presented in town – so if you're passing, drop in.

Serves 4 as a starter

200g pork belly, rind and excess fat removed
1 litre water
1 large carrot, cut into quarters lengthways and then into 2cm long pieces
200g new potatoes, peeled and cut into 2cm pieces
2 shitake mushrooms, thinly sliced
50g miso paste (white or barley)

To serve:
1 spring onion, finely sliced

Put the pork belly piece in the freezer, lying it flat on a chopping board for 45 minutes–1 hour to harden (this makes slicing it thinly much easier!). Slice the belly into 3mm thick strips and set aside in a bowl.

Bring the water to simmering point in a large saucepan and add the carrot, potatoes, mushrooms and pork slices. Allow to simmer very gently for 20 minutes, skimming off any scum and impurities that rise to the surface, until the potatoes are cooked and the carrots tender.

Stir in the miso paste and serve in bowls sprinkled with spring onion. Simple!

KASHMIRI LAMB
with yogurt and ginger

Serves 4

6 tbsp sunflower oil
1kg lamb shoulder, trimmed of any
excess fat and cut into 3–4cm cubes
3 bay leaves
4 cloves
8 cardamom pods
1 cinnamon stick, broken in two
1 onion, finely diced
1 hot long green chilli,
finely sliced (with seeds)
7cm piece of fresh ginger,
peeled and finely chopped

7 garlic cloves, chopped
1 tsp turmeric
1 tsp ground coriander
2 tsp ground cumin
3 tsp sweet paprika
8 tbsp full-fat natural yogurt
350ml water
1 tsp salt
3 tbsp toasted flaked almonds,
(toast them under a hot grill for
3–4 minutes until golden brown)

Preheat the oven to 160°C/325°F/Fan 150°C/gas mark 3, or you can cook on the hob if you prefer. Heat the oil in a deep, flameproof casserole dish that has a lid. Brown the lamb in batches for about 3–4 minutes and set aside in a bowl.

In the same pan, which should still have some oil left in it, add the bay leaves, cloves, cardamom pods and the cinnamon stick. Cook on a low heat for a minute or so until the bay leaves start to turn golden. Throw in the onion and chilli with its seeds (this is where the heat lies!) and cook gently for 10–12 minutes or until the onion begins to turn golden around the edges.

Meanwhile, pound the ginger and garlic to a pulp using a mortar and pestle. Once the onions have turned golden, add the garlic and ginger pulp to the pan and cook gently for 3–4 minutes, stirring regularly. Add all the remaining ground spices and cook for a couple of minutes to release their flavours. Tip the lamb and all its juices back into the pan and stir to ensure all the spices are combined with the meat. Mix 1 tablespoon of yogurt into the lamb and spices. Once it's completely incorporated, you can add the rest, a spoonful at a time, mixing well between additions. (Adding the yogurt slowly prevents it curdling.)

Finally, add the water and salt, bring to simmering point, cover with a lid and pop in the oven for 1½ hours, or continue cooking it gently on the hob for the same length of time, if you prefer. You want a thick sauce at the end, so if it hasn't reduced enough, simply cook it on the hob for a few minutes with the lid off until it reaches the desired consistency.

Serve sprinkled with toasted almonds and some plain pilau rice.

BEEF RENDANG

The beef in this classic dry curry from south-east Asia is slowly cooked in a bath of coconut milk and spices to create beautifully tender meat enveloped in an aromatic rich sauce.

Serves 4

For the curry paste:
6 long dried red chillies, deseeded
1 tsp cumin seeds
1 tsp coriander seeds
1 onion, chopped
1 tbsp finely chopped fresh ginger
1 tbsp finely chopped galangal
5 garlic cloves, roughly chopped
2 tbsp finely chopped lemongrass
2 tsp turmeric
3 tbsp water

For the curry:
40g unsweetened desiccated coconut
3 tbsp sunflower oil
3 cloves
1 cinnamon stick, broken in two
seeds from 6 cardamom pods
2 star anise
1kg chuck steak, cut into 3–4cm pieces
400ml tin coconut milk
150ml water
5 kaffir lime leaves, finely sliced (or 1 tbsp grated lime zest)
1 tbsp sugar
2 tsp tamarind paste (or 1 tbsp lime juice)
salt

To serve:
fresh coriander

Cover the chillies with boiling water and leave to soak for about 15 minutes.

Heat a heavy small frying pan on the hob, and when it's hot, tip in the desiccated coconut and gently cook, stirring frequently, for 3–4 minutes until golden brown. Set aside in a bowl for later.

Now make the curry paste. First roast the cumin and coriander seeds in the pan you used for the coconut. Roast the spices on a medium heat for about 2 minutes or so until the aromas are released and the cumin starts to change colour a little. Allow them to cool, then crush using a mortar and pestle. Drain the reconstituted chillies and chop them up roughly. Put these in a small blender along with the ground cumin and coriander and all the other curry paste ingredients and combine to a pulp.

In a wok that has a lid, or a heavy based saucepan, heat the sunflower oil. When it's hot, add the cloves, cinnamon stick, cardamom seeds and star anise. Cook these gently for 2–3 minutes to release their flavours.

Add the curry paste and cook for 4–5 minutes until the colour has darkened and the mixture dried a little. Throw in your pieces of beef and cook on a high heat to brown them. After about 5 minutes, when all the meat should be nicely browned, pour in the coconut milk, water, kaffir lime leaves, toasted coconut, sugar, tamarind paste (or lime juice) and some salt to taste.

Cook gently with the lid on for 1½–2 hours or until the sauce has nearly all dried up and the meat is tender, stirring regularly. If it's not looking dry enough, remove the lid and cook until you're happy with the consistency.

Serve garnished with fresh coriander.

BEEF MASSAMAN CURRY

This is another Thai curry inspired by David Thompson, the Australian chef, restaurateur and cookery writer, known for his expertise in Thai cuisine. The curry should be sweet, sour and salty, thanks to the mix of tamarind (or lime), sugar and fish sauce in the recipe.

Serves 4

For the curry paste:
10 long dried red chillies, deseeded
40g peanuts (without husks)
40g unsweetened desiccated coconut
3 bay leaves
5 cloves
6 cardamom pods
generous pinch of salt
1–2 tsp water

For the curry:
4 x 400ml tins coconut milk
600g beef chuck steak, cut into 3–4cm pieces
40g roasted peanuts
3 tbsp finely chopped fresh ginger
1 cinnamon stick
2 tbsp fish sauce
2 tbsp sugar
1 tsp tamarind paste, mixed with 4 tbsp water
or 3 tbsp lime juice

To serve:
fresh coriander

Pour the coconut milk over the beef in a heavy based saucepan. Bring to simmering point and cook gently for 2 hours, stirring occasionally until the beef is tender.

Pour boiling water over the dried chillies and leave to soak for up to 30 minutes. Preheat the oven to 190°C/375°F/Fan 180°C/gas mark 5 while you drain and roughly chop the chillies with a pair of scissors.

Now roast the peanuts for the paste and for the curry. Tip all the peanuts onto a baking tray and place in the hot oven for 10 minutes until they have turned golden brown. Keep an eye on them as you don't want them to burn. Remove and allow to cool.

Heat a dry pan on the hob and tip in the dessicated coconut. Stir continuously and cook gently for about 3–4 minutes until it turns golden. Set aside in a bowl for later.

Heat the pan you used for the coconut and add the bay leaves, cloves and cardamom pods. Stir regularly. After about 2 minutes the bay leaves will have started to turn darker and light brown around the edges. Transfer them to a mortar and pestle. Continue cooking the other spices for a few more minutes until the fragrances are released. Now tip them into the mortar, too, and allow to cool.

Remove the seeds from the roasted cardamom pods, discard the husks and grind with the bay leaves and cloves to a fine powder. Next add half of the roasted peanuts, continuing to grind to break them up. Once coarsely ground, add the chopped reconstituted chillies and salt. Continue to pound the ingredients together, adding the water when things get a little dry. Now tip in the toasted coconut and continue to pound with the pestle until you've got as smooth a paste as possible. (Apart from the spice grinding, all this pounding can, of course, be done in a small blender.)

When the beef is tender, drain the cooking liquor, reserving it for later, and put the beef, curry paste, peanuts, chopped ginger and cinnamon stick into the pan used for cooking the beef. Cook on a low flame, stirring regularly, for 3–4 minutes until the spices become aromatic.

Now return the beef cooking liquor to the pan and add the fish sauce, sugar and tamarind and water (or lime juice) mixture. Cook for a further 5 minutes, stirring regularly. Taste to make sure it's well balanced and equally sweet, salty and sour.

Serve sprinkled with fresh coriander alongside plain rice and, ideally, a Thai salad.

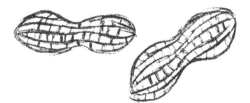

VIETNAMESE BEEF PHO

Vietnamese food has incredibly fresh and vibrant flavours thanks to the use of a multitude of fresh herbs. 'Pho' is one of the country's national dishes. In this recipe, a hot, aromatic broth is poured over noodles and strips of thinly sliced raw beef and served with fresh herbs, beansprouts, noodles and chilli.

Making the broth does take some time but it is delicious and the dish won't be the same if you buy ready-made stock.

Serves 4

For the broth:
3 onions
100g fresh ginger, unpeeled
2kg beef shin with bone
(ask your butcher to slice it into 3–4cm thick pieces)
2 carrots, peeled and chopped into large chunks
5 litres water
5 star anise
7 cloves
1 cinnamon stick
1 tsp black peppercorns
4 tbsp fish sauce
1 tbsp salt

For the bowls:
300g thick flat rice noodles, *bahn pho*
(if you can't find these, use any other rice noodle)
250g beef sirloin or fillet
3 tbsp roughly chopped coriander leaves
1 spring onion, finely sliced

To serve:
bunch of fresh coriander
bunch of fresh mint
bunch of fresh Thai basil
red-hot bird's eye chillies, thinly sliced
beansprouts
lime wedges

First, remove any loose skins from the onions and place them, along with the ginger, under a hot grill for 15–20 minutes. Turn the onions and ginger fairly frequently – the skins will blister and turn black in parts; this is absolutely fine as you'll be releasing some of the sweetness from the onions which will impart their flavour on the broth. Allow to cool before removing the onion skins, roughly peeling the ginger and giving it a bash with a rolling pin to bruise it.

Place the beef shin in a large, deep saucepan and cover with cold water. Bring to the boil, then simmer for a few minutes until scum rises to the surface. Drain the shin, give the bones a rinse under the cold tap to remove any more impurities and give the pan a quick scrub. Return the beef bones to the clean pan, cover with the 5 litres of fresh water and slowly bring to simmering point. Throw in the peeled grilled onions, the ginger and the carrots.

In a dry pan on the hob, roast the star anise, cloves, cinnamon stick and black peppercorns for a couple of minutes until the colours of the spices darken a little and you can smell the aromas being released. Add the roasted spices to the beef, carrots and water. Add the fish sauce and salt to the broth and allow to simmer, very gently, for 3–4 hours, depending on how much time you have.

Strain the broth; the meat from the beef shin should still be quite tasty so pull this off the bone and set aside. Keep the broth warm on the stove. Cook the noodles following the instructions on the packet. Whilst you're waiting for the noodles, thinly slice the beef (as thin as you dare!).

Now assemble the pho. Place a heap of noodles on the bottom of each of 4 large soup bowls, followed by several strips of beef and scatter around some pieces of the reserved cooked shin. Ladle the broth over the top, submerging the beef to cook it. Finally, sprinkle coriander leaves and sliced spring onions on top.

Serve fresh coriander, mint, Thai basil, sliced chillies, beansprouts and wedges of lime in bowls on the side for people to take as they please.

FISH STEW
with chilli, spinach and red peppers

This is a light fish stew made aromatic with spices. It works best using fresh tomatoes that are plump, juicy and perfectly ripe.

Serves 4

4 tbsp olive oil
2 bay leaves
1 tsp cumin seed
1 onion, finely sliced
1½cm piece of fresh ginger,
peeled and finely chopped
2 garlic cloves, finely chopped
1 medium–hot red chilli,
finely sliced (with seeds)
1 red pepper, finely sliced

1 tsp ground cumin
1 tsp ground coriander
¼ tsp chilli powder
1 tsp sweet paprika
1 tsp turmeric
500g ripe tomatoes, roughly chopped
250ml vegetable stock
salt
750g fillet of cod, cut into chunks
100g baby spinach

Heat the oil in a saucepan that has a lid, then throw in the bay leaves and cumin seed. After 30–40 seconds the bay leaf should darken and the cumin should start to pop. At this point, add the onion, ginger, garlic and chilli as well as the red pepper. Cook these for about 10 minutes on a moderate heat until the onions start to brown and the peppers soften.

Add all the spices and cook for a couple of minutes, stirring occasionally. Add the chopped tomatoes, stock and about 1 teaspoon of salt and cook gently, uncovered, for 30–40 minutes or until the sauce has thickened.

Season the fish with some salt. Put a layer of spinach over the thickened spicy tomato sauce to create a kind of platform and sit the pieces of fish on top. Cover the pan with a lid and cook for about 5 minutes until the fish has been steamed by the bubbling liquid underneath.

Serve straight away with some plain basmati rice or chapattis.

STICKY SPARE RIBS

There's something really satisfying about gnawing your way through a pile of ribs and making a complete mess of yourself in the process. Feel free to add some fresh or dried chilli to the mix if you like it a bit spicier, as this recipe only has a hint of heat in the sweet chilli sauce. If you have trouble finding *ketjap manis*, or Indonesian soy sauce, simply replace it with traditional dark soy sauce.

Serves 4

4 tbsp dark soy sauce
2 tbsp ketjap manis (Indonesian soy sauce)
1 tbsp tomato purée
4 garlic cloves, crushed
1 tbsp grated fresh ginger
2 tbsp Chinese rice wine or dry sherry
6 tbsp honey
2 tbsp sweet chilli sauce
2kg pork ribs (either in slabs or as individual ribs)

To serve:
2–3 spring onions, finely sliced

Preheat the oven to 160°C/325°F/Fan 150°C/gas mark 3. Simply mix together all the ingredients except the ribs in a large bowl to create a marinade. Add the ribs and smear the marinade all over them. If you're not in a rush, leave them to marinate for a few hours or overnight, but you'll get away with it if you cook them straight away.

Pour the ribs and all the marinade into a wide roasting tin so that they are no more than two deep. Pop them into the oven and cook for 1¼–1½ hours.

Every 15 minutes or so, move the ribs around and brush them with the sauce that collects at the base of the pan. Make sure they all get their fair share of time on the top layer! The sauce will eventually turn thick and sticky and the ribs will be shiny, caramelised at the edges and smell gorgeous!

Serve in piles sprinkled with finely sliced spring onions.

SWEET POTATO DHAL
with cherry tomatoes and coriander

This vegetarian curry (page 109, top) has a lovely fresh taste to it, thanks to the addition of fresh coriander and cherry tomatoes just before serving.

Serves 4–6

250g yellow split peas, rinsed and drained
3 cloves
6 cardamom pods
5 tbsp sunflower oil
2 onions, finely sliced
8cm piece of fresh ginger, peeled and grated
8 garlic cloves, crushed
1–2 small green chillies, thinly sliced (with seeds)
¼ tsp ground cinnamon

1 tsp sweet paprika
1 tsp ground cumin
1 tsp ground coriander
½ tsp turmeric
400g tin chopped tomatoes
250ml water
salt
500g sweet potato, peeled and cut into 2cm pieces
juice of ½ lemon
6 tbsp chopped fresh coriander
8 ripe cherry tomatoes, halved

Put the split peas in a pan and cover with cold water. Bring to the boil and simmer for 35 minutes–1 hour until tender and starting to break down. (They can vary a lot depending on when they were harvested.) Once cooked, drain and set aside.

Cook the cloves and cardamom pods in a heavy based frying pan for a couple of minutes until you can smell their aromas. Allow to cool, then remove the seeds from the cardamom pods, discarding the husks. Grind the spices using a mortar and pestle.

Heat the oil in a separate pan and when hot add the onions and cook for 10–12 minutes until soft and starting to brown, then add the ginger, garlic and chillies. Continue to cook gently for about 5 minutes. Add the toasted spices with the cinnamon, paprika, cumin, coriander and turmeric, stir thoroughly and cook gently for a couple of minutes before adding the tomatoes and letting it simmer for another 2–3 minutes.

Add the water, some salt and the sweet potato chunks. Bring back to simmering point, cover with a lid and allow to cook gently for 25–30 minutes or until the sweet potato is soft.

Stir through the cooked split peas, bringing everything back up to heat again. Mix in the lemon juice, coriander and cherry tomatoes. Have a taste and add more salt if you think it's needed.

MIDDLE EAST
& AFRICA

PERSIAN CHICKEN STEW
with sour cherries and walnuts

I love sweet and sour flavours, and when I discovered pomegranate molasses and sour cherries a couple of years ago I was in my element. I was certain they could form part of a stew – I just had to work out what! I toyed around with a lamb and pomegranate stew but it wasn't quite right … In my quest to find the right balance I stumbled across *fesenjun*, a classic Persian dish of duck or chicken with a pomegranate and walnut sauce (page 129). I had my inspiration! This is a rich, luxurious stew that goes perfectly with some simple brown rice or bulgur wheat with a little lemon juice and olive oil running through.

There are a few different brands of pomegranate molasses on the market and some are sweeter than others. You want real acidity in this dish, so if you think it's a bit too sweet, squeeze some lemon juice in at the end to perfect this stunner.

Serves 4

130g walnuts
20g unsalted butter
2½ tbsp olive oil
2 onions, finely sliced
1 garlic clove, crushed
½ tsp turmeric
¼ tsp ground cinnamon
75g dried sour cherries
8 boneless and skinless chicken thighs
or 4 boneless and skinless breasts
(about 1kg), cut into 3–4cm pieces
4 tbsp pomegranate molasses
500ml chicken stock or water
salt and black pepper
lemon juice (if needed)

To serve:
3–4 tbsp pomegranate seeds
chopped fresh parsley

Preheat the oven to 190°C/375°F/Fan 180°C/gas mark 5. Spread the walnuts over a baking tray and roast for 10–15 minutes until they're starting to colour and smoke a little. Watch them like a hawk – you want coloured, not burnt! Take them out of the oven and leave them to cool a bit. Grind them in a blender or, if you're feeling strong, use a mortar and pestle. You want to get them pretty fine and starting to turn a little buttery.

Meanwhile, heat the butter and olive oil in a large saucepan or flameproof casserole dish on the hob. Add the onions to the pan and cook gently for about 20 minutes with the lid on, stirring occasionally until they're very soft but not turning brown. Once they're soft, add the garlic and cook for a couple more minutes. Throw in the turmeric, cinnamon and sour cherries – this bit smells great! Cook on a medium heat for a couple of minutes then add the chicken to the pan. Turn up the heat a little and cook the chicken in the spices and onions until it's sealed – about 5 minutes.

Add the pomegranate molasses to the pan with the ground walnuts. Give everything a good stir, then add the stock or water along with a few grinds of black pepper and some salt. Bring to simmering point, then lower the flame and cook for about 15 minutes with the lid on, giving it a stir from time to time until the chicken is cooked through. Season to taste and give it a squeeze of lemon juice if you think it needs it.

Serve with some brown rice and with some pomegranate seeds and chopped parsley scattered over. An all-time favourite!

TUNISIAN CHICKEN STEW
with harissa and caraway

I think spicy harissa paste (made from red chillies) is delicious simply spread thinly on some good bread. Here, though, it gives a kick to a rich tomato sauce that is fragrant with caraway seed (page 128, top). You can buy harissa paste in large supermarkets – look out for the brand Belazu, they do a 'rose' harissa which, I think, is especially good.

Serves 4

2 tbsp olive oil
8 chicken thighs
(about 1kg in total), skin on
salt and freshly ground black pepper
2 onions, finely sliced
2 garlic cloves, finely chopped
½ tsp turmeric
1 tsp caraway seeds
½ tsp ground cinnamon
2–3 tbsp harissa paste (add more if you like it spicier)

400g tin chopped tomatoes
100ml water
200g cooked haricot beans (optional)

For the mint yogurt:
2 tbsp finely chopped fresh mint
6 tbsp plain yogurt

To serve:
chopped fresh parsley

Heat the oil in a wide frying pan or heavy saucepan that has a lid and is big enough to hold all the chicken in one layer. Season the chicken with salt and black pepper then brown them in the oil, skin-side down, for 5–7 minutes until golden and crisp. Flip them over and seal the other side for a minute or so and transfer to a plate. (It is easiest to do this in batches.)

In the same pan, gently fry the onions for about 5 minutes until soft, then stir in the garlic, turmeric, caraway seeds and cinnamon and cook gently, stirring, for a couple more minutes. Add the harissa paste – you should now get a wonderful aroma of chillies and caraway and everything will turn a lovely shade of red. Continue to cook gently for another 2 minutes, to release all the flavours from the spices. Add the tomatoes along with the water, some black pepper and a few pinches of salt. Then push the chicken, skin-side up, into the mixture. Cover with the lid and cook gently for 30 minutes until the chicken is tender.
Meanwhile, make the mint yogurt by simply mixing the chopped mint into the yogurt.

Once the chicken has been cooking for 30 minutes, add the haricot beans, if using, scattering them around the chicken thighs and allowing them to heat through in the sauce.

Serve the chicken sprinkled with some chopped parsley and accompanied by a spoonful of mint yogurt.

FISH TAGINE
with olives and preserved lemons

This recipe is packed full of Moroccan flavours and is a complete meal in itself.

Serves 4

4 tbsp olive oil
1 medium onion, finely sliced
2 tbsp coriander stalks, finely chopped
5 garlic cloves, finely chopped
1 red pepper, cut into ½cm slices
2 celery sticks, cut into ½cm slices
½ bulb fennel, finely sliced
½ tsp ground ginger
¼ tsp ground cumin
¼ tsp ground sweet paprika
¼ tsp cayenne pepper
1 cinnamon stick, broken into two
45g preserved lemons,
skin and pulp finely chopped

60g green olives
200g ripe chopped tomatoes
300ml water
salt
650g waxy potatoes,
peeled and diced into 3cm chunks
**750g firm white fish (cod, pollock,
coley, monkfish or John Dory)**,
cut into 8–10cm pieces (leave the skin
on all but monkfish to help the flesh stay
together during the cooking)
2 tbsp chopped fresh parsley
2 tbsp chopped fresh coriander

In a wide saucepan that has a lid, heat the oil and gently cook the onion for 10 minutes until softened. Add the coriander stalks, garlic, red pepper, celery and fennel. Continue to cook gently with the lid on for about 20 minutes or so until the vegetables are soft.

Add the ginger, cumin, paprika, cayenne pepper and cinnamon stick to the pan, stirring well to incorporate them, then cook for a couple of minutes to release their flavours. Stir in the chopped preserved lemons and the olives.

Now add the tomatoes to the pan followed by the water and some salt. Mix it all around before plopping in the potatoes and cooking with the lid on for 20–30 minutes until the potatoes are soft. At this point, push the pieces of fish into the cooking vegetables, cover with the lid once again and cook for a further 5–10 minutes until the fish is just cooked.

Sprinkle with the chopped parsley and coriander and serve.

GHANAIAN CHICKEN AND PEANUT STEW

This recipe is adapted from one kindly given to me by Adwoa from the Jollof Pot, who are regulars on the London food-market scene, specialising in fantastic Ghanaian food.

The dish works really well served alongside some slices of cucumber, which will cut through the heat of the chilli and also the richness of the peanut butter.

Serves 4

4 tbsp olive oil
8 chicken thighs (about 1kg in total)
salt and freshly ground black pepper
1 red onion, thinly sliced
3 garlic cloves, finely chopped
3cm ginger, peeled and finely chopped
1 Scotch bonnet chilli or 2 other hot chillies (Scotch bonnet are very hot!)

2 bay leaves
2 tsp sweet paprika
200g tin chopped tomatoes
150g chunky peanut butter
250ml chicken stock

Heat the oil in a heavy based pan that has a lid and will hold all the chicken thighs. Season the chicken with salt and black pepper and then brown in the hot oil on a moderate heat, skin-side down, for 5–7 minutes until nicely golden. Turn the thighs over, seal the other side for a couple of minutes and set them aside in a bowl. You'll probably need to do this in 2 batches.

Add the onion to the pan and cook gently for about 5 minutes until it has started to soften. Add the garlic, ginger, chilli and bay leaves and continue to cook gently for about 5 minutes until the onions are completely soft.

Remove the pan from the heat and stir in the paprika. Add the tomatoes and return the pan to the heat. Cook for a couple of minutes before stirring in the peanut butter and stock, some salt and black pepper. Make sure the peanut butter is completely mixed in as it can seem quite gloopy and hard to incorporate.

Return the browned chicken thighs to the pan, skin-side up, and cover the pan with the lid. Gently cook the chicken for 25–30 minutes until tender. Ensure you stir it regularly to prevent anything sticking to the base of the pan (the peanut butter has a tendency to sink and stick, so you need to be careful!).

Check for seasoning then serve with some plain brown rice and some thick slices of cucumber dressed with a little olive oil, lemon juice, salt and black pepper.

DUCK AND GINGER STEW

I've adapted this recipe from one in Keith Floyd's *Floyd on Africa*. It's an interesting way to cook duck, clearly drawing on the French tradition of 'confit', where duck or goose is cooked slowly in fat. Here the duck is cooked slowly in water and then cooked for a second time with tomatoes, ginger and garlic.

Serves 4

4 duck legs, thighs still attached (around 200g each)
1kg ripe tomatoes
4 tbsp olive oil
2 red onions, finely sliced
40g ginger, very finely sliced
10 garlic cloves, crushed
salt and freshly ground black pepper

Place the duck legs in a saucepan large enough to hold them in one layer, then cover them with 1–1½ litres of water (the amount depends on how big your pot is – they need to be covered). Bring to a simmer and cook the duck legs slowly for 1–1½ hours until they are tender.

Meanwhile, skin the tomatoes. Simply plunge them into a bowl of boiling water for about a minute and then cool them under cold running water. The skins will then easily slip off. Roughly chop the tomato flesh, making sure you keep all the juices.

Drain the duck legs and place them on a plate. Heat the olive oil in the same pan, add the onions and ginger and cook slowly for about 10 minutes until the onions have softened. Add the garlic and continue to cook slowly for another 5 minutes, by which time the onions will be very soft and the ginger nicely cooked.

Add the chopped tomatoes to the pan, bring everything to simmering point and cook gently for a further 10 minutes until the tomatoes are breaking down. Season with some salt and black pepper and then add the duck legs to the pot. Cook gently for a further 30–40 minutes until the tomatoes have reduced to a thick pulp that coats the duck. If the duck looks to be breaking down and falling apart before the sauce is thick enough, remove to a plate so that the sauce can reduce further.

Taste the sauce for seasoning and add a little more salt if you think it's needed.

HARIRA

This is one of those halfway houses between a soup and a stew, but I think it's thick enough to warrant being in this book!

Harira is usually eaten during the holy Muslim month of Ramadan to break the fasting day. It's a rich, thick, soupy stew of lamb, lentils, chickpeas and a host of spices and fresh herbs. Enjoy it on a chilly night with a hunk of bread.

Serves 4–6

500g diced lamb shoulder, trimmed of as much fat as possible and cut into 1cm pieces
2 litres water
125g green lentils, rinsed
3 tbsp olive oil
2 onions, finely chopped
½ tsp turmeric
½ tsp ground ginger
¼ tsp ground cinnamon

½ tsp freshly ground black pepper
400g tin chopped tomatoes
1 tsp salt
300g tinned or cooked chickpeas
20g plain flour
50g vermicelli noodles, broken into small pieces
4 tbsp chopped fresh coriander
4 tbsp chopped fresh parsley
juice of 1 lemon

Put the meat into a large heavy based saucepan and pour over the water. Bring to simmering point and skim off any impurities that rise to the surface. Continue to simmer for around 5 minutes until no more scum is rising to the surface, then add the lentils.

In a separate pan, heat the oil and cook the onions gently for about 15 minutes until they are golden brown. Add the spices and black pepper and cook for 2 minutes, stirring well. Add the tomatoes and cook for 5 minutes until they have turned pulpy, then pour this mixture into the bubbling lamb and water. Add the salt and cook gently on the hob for 1 hour.

After the hour, add the chickpeas to the pan and continue cooking for a further 30 minutes.

Mix the flour to a paste the thickness of double cream with a little water and add this to the bubbling stew, stirring all the time to avoid any lumps forming. Add the broken vermicelli noodles and cook gently for a further 5 minutes until the noodles are cooked and the flour has been cooked through.

Finish by stirring through the chopped herbs and lemon juice. Taste for seasoning and serve simply with some crusty bread and more fresh herbs, if you wish.

PERSIAN LAMB AND QUINCE STEW

This simple stew is quite delicate in flavour and very easy to prepare. Quinces are similar to apples but have a firmer, grainier texture and are much more acidic, and when cooked their flesh turns a lovely pale pink colour. If you can't get hold of quinces, an acidic apple, such as a Granny Smith, would work well in this dish – but don't add them until 15 minutes before the end of the cooking time.

Serves 4–6

3 tbsp olive oil
2 onions, roughly chopped
2 garlic cloves, finely chopped
1 tsp ground ginger
1 tsp turmeric
¼ tsp cinnamon
¼ tsp ground allspice
¼ tsp ground nutmeg
1kg lamb shoulder, trimmed of any
excess fat and cut into 2–3cm pieces
500ml water

salt
100g yellow split peas,
rinsed and drained
2 quinces, peeled, cored and cut
into 16 pieces
sugar (optional)

To serve:
chopped fresh parsley

Heat the oil in a heavy based, flameproof casserole dish that has a lid and soften the onions in the oil for 10–12 minutes until they are starting to brown at the edges. Add the garlic and spices and continue to cook gently for a further 2 minutes before adding the lamb.

Preheat the oven to 160°C/325°F/Fan 150°C/gas mark 3 (or you can cook the stew on the hob). Cook the lamb on a moderate heat for about 5 minutes, stirring often, until the meat is completely sealed and has been well incorporated into the spices and onions. Then add the water and a few pinches of salt. Cook very gently on the hob or in the oven for 1 hour.

Add the split peas to the pan and continue to cook gently for a further 30 minutes. Stir in the quinces and cook for a further 30 minutes. You're looking for a really thick stew, so now's the time to remove the lid to drive off a little more of the water. Taste for seasoning – you may well need to add more salt at this stage and a little sugar if your quinces are especially sour.

Serve sprinkled with chopped parsley on some simple saffron rice.

LAMB TAGINE
with apricots, raisins and honey

This dish gets its name from the tagine pot in which it is traditionally cooked, which is a wide pan with a conical-shaped lid that has a hole in the top to let the steam out. If you don't have a tagine, use a wide saucepan with a lid that allows steam to escape. You're still allowed to call the dish a tagine, though!

This recipe uses a classic spice mix to create a beautifully aromatic dish that you'll find hard to wait for. Try experimenting with different dried fruits to make this your own.

Serves 4

2 tbsp olive oil
2 onions, roughly chopped
3 garlic cloves, finely chopped
2 tsp sweet paprika
2 tsp ground ginger
1 tsp ground coriander
1 tsp ground cumin
1 tsp turmeric
½ tsp ground allspice
½ tsp cayenne pepper
pinch of saffron
2 cinnamon sticks
900g lamb shoulder, trimmed of as much fat as possible
and diced into 3–4cm pieces
400g tin tomatoes
1 tbsp honey
1 handful of raisins (about 30g)
100g dried apricots
25g flaked almonds
300ml water
salt and freshly ground black pepper
125g cooked chickpeas (tinned are fine), drained and rinsed

To serve:
chopped fresh parsley

Heat the oil in a wide saucepan that has a lid and cook the onions gently for 10–15 minutes until soft and starting to brown. Then add the garlic and all the spices – including the cinnamon sticks – and continue to cook for a couple of minutes to let the spices release all their great flavours.

Next throw in the lamb pieces and cook for 5–8 minutes until all the meat has sealed and the spices have begun to work their way into the flesh. (I've read so many tagine recipes – some brown the meat before cooking the onions and others don't. However, I think you get as good a result without browning the meat first; after all, there are so many flavours in this tagine that it can do without the caramelised flavour of browned meat that is so key in other classic stews.)

Add the tomatoes, honey, raisins, apricots, almonds and water. Grind over a generous helping of black pepper and a few good pinches of salt and stir everything together. Cover with the lid but allow a little steam to escape. Cook gently on the hob for 1½ hours.

Add the chickpeas and continue cooking, still allowing some steam to escape, for another 30 minutes. Test for seasoning and adjust if you think it needs it. The stew should be lovely and thick, so if it's not quite there yet, remove the lid completely and cook for a little longer.

Serve with bulgur wheat or couscous and sprinkle with chopped parsley.

ARMENIAN LAMB STEW

This is a really simple stew to make and the spices will fill your home with great aromas as it cooks away.

Serves 4

3 tbsp olive oil
900g lamb shoulder,
trimmed of as much fat as possible
and cut into 2–3cm pieces
salt and freshly ground black pepper
2 onions, roughly chopped
3 garlic cloves, finely chopped
2 carrots, peeled and roughly chopped

2 tsp cumin seeds
½ tsp ground allspice
½ tsp cayenne pepper
1 tbsp flour
2 tbsp tomato purée
1 red pepper, sliced into 1cm strips
400ml beef stock
1 glass red wine (about 175ml)

Preheat the oven to 160°C/325°F/Fan 150°C/gas mark 3, or you can use the hob. Heat the olive oil in a heavy based, flameproof casserole dish that has a lid. Brown the lamb for about 5 minutes in batches, seasoning with black pepper as you go. Set aside in a bowl.

Throw the onions, garlic and carrots into the pan with a little more oil, if necessary, and a splash of water if the pan is very dry. Scrape up the bits from the bottom of the pan and cook gently for 8–10 minutes until the onions have softened.

Add the cumin seeds, allspice, cayenne pepper and the flour to the pan, stirring to incorporate them well. Cook for a couple more minutes to release all the flavours from the spices.

Add the tomato purée, red pepper, stock and red wine to the pan along with some black pepper and a few good pinches of salt. Now return the browned lamb and any juices that may have collected to the pan. Cover with the lid and pop in the oven or cook gently on the hob for about 2 hours until the lamb is tender. If it's looking like there's a little too much liquid left, remove the lid 30 minutes before the cooking time is up to allow the sauce to thicken and reduce a little.

Check for seasoning and serve with a rice pilaf.

CHICKPEA AND SWEET POTATO TAGINE

Feel free to replace the sweet potato with the same weight of butternut squash in this fragrant vegetarian stew (page 128, bottom).

Serves 4–6

3 tbsp olive oil
1 red onion, cut into 8 segments
3 garlic cloves, finely chopped
½ tsp ground ginger
1 tsp ground cinnamon
1 tsp sweet paprika
2 tsp ground cumin
1 tsp ground coriander
2 good pinches of saffron threads
1 pinch of cayenne pepper
200g tin chopped tomatoes
250ml vegetable stock

1 tsp tomato purée
salt and freshly ground black pepper
1 carrot, peeled and cut into ½cm slices
400g sweet potato, peeled and cut
into 2cm pieces
100g dried apricots
240g tin chickpeas, drained
juice and grated zest of 1 lemon

To serve:
4 tbsp chopped fresh coriander

Heat the olive oil in a wide pan that has a lid, add the onion and cook gently for 10 minutes until soft and some of the pieces are starting to turn brown at the edges. Add the garlic and all the spices and cook gently for a couple of minutes, stirring to avoid the spices burning but allowing them to release their flavours.

Add the tomatoes, stock and tomato purée. Stir through a few generous pinches of salt and some twists of the pepper mill. Now add the carrot, sweet potato, apricots and chickpeas. Bring to simmering point, cover with the lid just at an angle to allow a little steam to escape and cook gently for about 30 minutes until the squash and carrots are tender.

Stir in the lemon juice and zest and taste for seasoning, adding more salt if you think it needs it. Sprinkle over the chopped coriander just before serving.

SPICY ETHIOPIAN BEEF STEW

A special blend of spices called *berbere* is essential for this stew – it is an aromatic and peppery blend of cloves, cayenne pepper, cardamom, allspice berries and black peppercorns. Luckily, I met Magali when I was selling stews in the markets, and she has acted as consultant spice guru for this dish. Magali owns Spice Mountain, which trades at Borough Market in London, selling a huge range of wonderful spice blends. The berbere recipe below will make about 10 tablespoons' worth of spice mix, which is enough for several batches of this stew.

Traditionally this dish would be served with a sour pancake called *injera*, which balances the spiciness of the stew. If you're not lucky enough to have a local Ethiopian source to supply you with these pancakes, serve this stew with plain basmati rice and perhaps some yogurt on the side. I also like to accompany this with some fresh chopped tomatoes and thinly sliced spring onions.

Stew serves 4–6

For the berbere spice mix:
4 tbsp cayenne pepper
1 tsp ground ginger
½ tsp ground cinnamon
3 tbsp sweet paprika
1 tsp cumin seeds
1 tsp cardamom seeds
(from around 20 cardamom pods)
7 allspice berries, roughly crushed
1 tsp fenugreek seeds
1 tsp coriander seeds
6 cloves
1 tsp black peppercorns

For the stew:
4 tbsp olive oil
2 onions, roughly chopped
2–3 tbsp berbere spice mix
(depending on how hot you like it)
5 garlic cloves, finely chopped
800g chuck steak, trimmed of any
excess fat and cut into 3–4cm pieces
2 x 400g tins tomatoes
1 tsp salt

To serve:
chopped fresh coriander
plain yogurt

First make the berbere spice mix. Heat a dry heavy based frying pan on the hob, then add the cayenne pepper, ginger, cinnamon and paprika to the pan and roast the spices on a low heat for a couple of minutes until they start to smoke slightly. Keep stirring the spices to ensure nothing burns. As soon as they start smoking, tip the spices into a bowl and set aside.

In the hot dry pan, add the cumin and cardamom seeds, crushed allspice berries, fenugreek and coriander seeds, cloves and black peppercorns. Roast them on a low heat for a couple of minutes, just until they start to smoke a little. Pour them immediately into a mortar and pestle or spice blender and allow them to cool before grinding to a powder. Combine all the spices and store in a sealed airtight jar. You now have your berbere spice mix!

Now make the stew. Heat the oil in a deep saucepan that has a lid and soften the onions. After about 10 minutes, once the onions are turning golden at the edges, add the berbere spice mix and garlic. Cook on a moderate heat for a couple of minutes, stirring continuously to ensure the spices and garlic don't burn.

Add all of the beef to the pan, mixing it well with the onions and spices. Cook on a moderate heat for 4–5 minutes until all the beef is sealed and coated well with spices. Makes sure you scrape the bottom of the pan to avoid anything burning. Add the tomatoes and a few pinches of salt. Bring to simmering point and allow to cook gently for 1½–2 hours with the lid slightly askew to allow some steam to escape. The stew is ready when the sauce has thickened and the beef is tender.

Taste for seasoning – you may need to add more salt to bring out the flavour of the spices. Serve sprinkled with chopped coriander and with some plain yogurt on the side.

ACCOMPANIMENTS

BOULANGÈRE POTATOES

This potato gratin dish is incredibly simple to make and extremely moreish.

Serves 4–6

40g butter
900g potatoes, thinly sliced (leave the skins on)
1 onion, finely chopped
salt and freshly ground black pepper
freshly grated nutmeg
450ml hot chicken or vegetable stock

Preheat the oven to 180°C/350°F/Fan 170°C/gas mark 4. Using a little of the butter, grease the base and sides of a 25cm x 25cm (or thereabouts) baking dish, then put a layer of sliced potatoes on the base followed by some of the chopped onion. Season with some salt, black pepper and a dusting of nutmeg.

Repeat the process another couple of times and finish with a layer of potatoes. (You can make the final layer look attractive if you overlap the slices, but I tend not to bother as I always manage to make a mess of it and have different-sized slices that don't quite work ...) Now push everything down firmly so it's as level as possible and then simply dot the remaining butter all over the top, season with a little more salt, black pepper and nutmeg and pour over the stock. Pop into the oven for 2 hours.

After about an hour of cooking, check to see that the potatoes aren't browning too quickly (as ovens do vary). If they're already quite golden, loosely cover with a piece of tin foil to protect the potatoes but still allow moisture to escape.

Continue cooking for the full 2 hours, by which time the liquid should have evaporated and you'll be left with crisp potatoes on the top and moist creamy ones underneath.

MASHED POTATO

This book would be missing something if there wasn't a recipe for some good mashed potato. There's nothing quite like the comforting feeling of eating a pile of mashed spuds with a stew ...

The trick is simply to use a good floury potato, such as a Maris Piper. If in doubt, ask in the greengrocer or look on the packet for advice. You just want to make sure you avoid waxy ones as these would go all sticky and gluey when you mash them.

Serves 4–6

1.3kg peeled floury potatoes, cut into 2cm cubes
salt and freshly ground black pepper
50g unsalted butter
50ml whole milk or cream

Tip the chopped potatoes in a deep saucepan, cover with water, add 1 teaspoon of salt and bring to the boil. Cook for about 15 minutes or until tender (timings will vary depending on the potato variety and how big you diced them!).

Once tender, drain in a colander and allow the potatoes to steam dry for a couple of minutes – you don't want any water going into your mash. Now simply mash with the butter and milk or cream until soft, creamy and smooth. Add some salt and black pepper to season.

Additions

- Season simply with a little nutmeg
- Stir in a little grated Cheddar and wholegrain mustard
- Stir in some red or green pesto
- Replace the butter with extra virgin olive oil
- For 'colcannon', fry some cooked Savoy cabbage and sliced leeks in butter, then mix into your mashed potatoes
- For 'champ', simply stir in some sliced spring onions
- Try adding a couple of tablespoons of hot horseradish cream with some chopped fresh mint and parsley

Sometimes it's nice simply to gently crush unpeeled cooked potatoes. Just as they are cooked, gently crush them with the back of a fork and add any of the above combinations.

The world is your oyster with the humble potato!

SAUTÉED POTATOES

I am truly a sautéed potato convert. They are delicious. Crunchy shells of crispy, buttery, golden addictiveness filled with light, fluffy, soft potato. Perfect for soaking up juices or for eating just on their own in a big bowl.

650g peeled floury potatoes (such as Maris Piper), cut into 2cm chunks
2 tbsp olive oil
25g unsalted butter
2 garlic cloves, finely chopped
salt and freshly ground black pepper
1 tbsp chopped fresh parsley

Plunge the peeled and chopped spuds into a pan of boiling salted water. Bring the water back to the boil and cook the potatoes rapidly for 7–8 minutes until the outer parts of the potato chunks have started to soften. Drain in a colander and allow them to steam so all the water evaporates.

Heat the olive oil in a large non-stick frying pan wide enough to fit all your potatoes in one layer. When the oil is good and hot, tip the drained potatoes into the pan and spread them out evenly. Cook the chunks on a moderate heat, without moving them, for 3–4 minutes until the underside is golden and crisp. Now turn them over and add the butter in small pieces to the pan.

Continue cooking the potatoes, turning them every couple of minutes so that each side is nicely golden and crisp.

After about 20 minutes the potatoes should be evenly golden and crisp on the outside and thoroughly cooked on the inside. Test one to make sure (you can always cook them a little longer if needs be). Next, throw the garlic into the pan with some salt and black pepper and give the pan a good shake. After a couple more minutes, add the parsley and immediately tip out into a serving bowl or onto warm plates.

Eat. They are incredibly addictive!

ROSEMARY AND GARLIC ROAST POTATOES

I'm certainly not the first to include a recipe for these in a cookery book; however, they're so good and so simple to prepare that it seems a shame not to.

650g new potatoes, halved (unpeeled)
3 tbsp olive oil
½ head garlic, around 6 cloves removed and bashed a little
leaves from 1 sprig of fresh rosemary
salt and freshly ground black pepper

Preheat the oven to 180°C/350°F/Fan 170°C/gas mark 4. Mix everything together and tip it all into a roasting tin big enough to hold the potatoes in a single layer. Chuck the tray in the oven to cook for about 1 hour 20 minutes. Give the tin a shake halfway through cooking.

The potatoes are ready when caramelised on the outside and completely soft on the inside. You'll just have to taste one to make sure they're done – it's a hard life being the cook!

RICE

Rice is a great accompaniment to so many stews; I'd either choose basmati, with its delicious fragrant flavour, or brown rice – always.

Cooking perfect rice to a point where it is fluffy and light is not as easy as you would think. There are 2 methods that I like to use. The first is how my mum has always cooked it – in the oven, covered with a lid. I think this is the easiest way by far. The other way I cook it is on the hob, which takes less time, but needs some attention. I am not a fan of boiling rice in a load of water and then rinsing it, as I find it ends up slimy and a little insipid.

There are two things I don't do to rice. I don't rinse it (I never think it needs it), nor do I add any salt to plain rice when cooking it. This is my personal choice. Feel free to add salt if you wish.

Plain basmati rice – for 4 generous portions

250g basmati rice
300ml boiling water, light chicken or vegetable stock

The oven method:

Preheat the oven to 180°C/350°F/Fan 170°C/gas mark 4. Put the rice into a small ovenproof pot that has a lid and pour over the boiling liquid. Cover with a lid. Cook in the oven for 35 minutes. Done!

The hob method:

Put the rice in a small saucepan on the hob and cover with the liquid. Without stirring, gently bring the liquid to simmering point. Now lower the heat, you only want a few bubbles to come to the surface so use the smallest flame if you need to. Cover with the lid and leave for 10 minutes, covered (and don't peek, not even once).

Remove the lid, give a brief gentle stir with a folding action to avoid any grains breaking up. You just want to let a little air circulate between the grains. Now cover again with the lid and leave for 10 minutes. Done!

Both methods should produce soft, fluffy rice.

Brown rices can vary enormously and need more water and cooking times. However, you can follow these general methodologies given above. If it looks like you need more water at any time, just add a little more, but make sure it's boiling water.

Adventures with rice

Once you've mastered cooking rice, you can be extremely creative with it and add flavourings. For the following ideas, only use basmati rice.

- For a fragrant rice to serve with curries, simply add a few cardamom pods, cloves, a cinnamon stick, a couple of bay leaves and a couple of pinches of turmeric when you're adding the liquid.
- Soften half a finely chopped onion in butter or olive oil with some cumin seeds and then add the rice to this before adding the water.
- For saffron rice, soften half a finely chopped onion in butter. Once soft, add a pinch of saffron strands. Then add the rice and liquid as above.
- For a tasty rice pilaf, build on saffron rice, adding some currants or sultanas to the mix as well as some flaked almonds and a few pine kernels.
- For something Mediterranean, soften onions in a pan with olive oil. Add sliced sundried tomatoes and chopped olives and some grated lemon zest.
- For a fruity rice, add dried sour cherries or cranberries to the rice before adding liquid.

The list could go on. Just be creative!

BULGUR WHEAT

I much prefer bulgur wheat to couscous; it has a coarser texture and a more pronounced, nutty flavour. Try to buy the coarsest you can find as I think this gives the best result.

There are umpteen ways of cooking bulgur wheat but I like simply to cover it in boiling water or stock and let it rest for about 20–30 minutes.

Serves 4

320g coarse bulgur wheat
600ml boiling water or stock
salt and freshly ground black pepper

Tip the bulgur wheat into a bowl – don't use too big a bowl as this will cool everything and the bulgur won't cook.

Now pour over the boiling water or stock. Immediately seal the bowl with clingfilm and leave for 20–30 minutes. Don't lift the clingfilm to have a peek! The bulgur wheat will absorb all the moisture and bulk up, though it should still have a little bite to it. Season with a little salt and black pepper.

Variations

- Stir in 2 tablespoons of extra virgin olive oil, a handful of roughly chopped fresh parsley and the grated zest and juice of 1 lemon.

- Gently cook a thinly sliced red onion, some dried sour cherries or dried cranberries in some butter for 10–15 minutes. Add some unsalted pistachio nuts and continue to cook for a couple more minutes. Add a couple of tablespoons of pomegranate molasses and then tip into the cooked plain bulgur wheat.

- In some melted butter, gently fry 1 onion, 8 chopped apricots, a few chopped sundried tomatoes and a teaspoon of cumin seed until the onions are soft. Mix this into some cooked bulgur wheat and squeeze over the juice and zest of a couple of lemons.

- Rather like rice, the possibilities are endless.

DUMPLINGS

There's something about the texture of dumplings that reminds me of being a child. Or it could be down to the fact that I always burn the roof of my mouth on them because I'm too impatient to wait for them to cool a little!

200g self-raising flour
100g suet (vegetable or beef)
½ tsp salt
1 tbsp finely chopped fresh parsley
150ml water

In a bowl, mix together the flour, suet and salt using your fingertips to break up the suet – you can do this in a food processor, too, of course. Mix in the parsley and then add the water to the dry ingredients, bringing it together with your hands until you've got a good dough consistency. Divide it to make 8–10 balls and set them aside, covered, to prevent them drying out.

Drop the dumplings onto your cooking stew for the final 30 minutes of its cooking time – make sure about half the dumpling sits below the liquid. Keep the lid on your pot so they cook in the steam generated from the stew below.

After 30 minutes, the dumplings will have puffed up. Now raise the temperature of your oven to 180°C/350°F/Fan 170°C/gas mark 4 and cook for a further 15 minutes or so until the dumplings have formed a golden crust. Alternatively, do this under the grill.

Variations

Be creative with this basic recipe – try adding any of the following combinations to the mix:

- Stilton and horseradish (see Beef in ale with horseradish and Stilton dumplings, page 38)
- Grated Cheddar and mustard
- Fresh herbs (thyme, rosemary, parsley, sage, tarragon)
- Goats' cheese and caramelised onions

PARMESAN POLENTA

I love the texture of polenta and it's easy to make, as long as you keep stirring, and keep stirring, and stirring ... The addition of truffle oil in the recipe is optional, but I think it adds a delicious earthy bit of luxury, which I'm always up for.

Serves 4–6

1 litre water/chicken or vegetable stock
250ml milk
50g unsalted butter
2 tsp salt
250g polenta
100g grated Parmesan
1 tbsp truffle oil (optional)

First bring the water or stock, milk, butter and salt to the boil in a pan set over a high heat. Now, whisking continuously with a balloon whisk to avoid any lumps forming (they can easily appear), pour the polenta into the liquid in an even stream (it might be easier to ask someone else to do the pouring as it's a bit like trying to pat your head at the same time as rubbing your stomach).

Continue whisking for a couple of minutes then lower the heat. Change to a wooden spoon and cook for a further 15–20 minutes, stirring constantly until the polenta starts to come away from the sides of the pan. If it feels like it's getting too thick too quickly, simply add a little boiling water.

When the polenta is ready, stir in the grated Parmesan and truffle oil, if using, and serve.

Tip – Another way to serve polenta is to pour the cooked mixture out into a greased baking tray, leave it to cool and then cut it into squares. These can then be grilled or fried in butter and served with a little more Parmesan grated on top.

INDEX

A

ale
- beef in, with horseradish and Stilton dumplings 38–9
- sausages and cabbage, with pot roast pheasant 34–5

anchovies, tomatoes and olives, with lamb 74

apples and prunes, with pork 48

apricots
- chickpea and sweet potato tagine 141
- raisins and honey with lamb tagine 137–9

asparagus, cider and tarragon, with chicken stew 30–1

aubergine, caponata 102–3

B

bacon, New England clam chowder 19

Barolo, beef braised in 89

beans, Boston baked 12–13

beef 8
- in ale, with horseradish and Stilton dumplings 38–9
- with beetroot and Stilton 47
- boeuf bourguignon 94
- braised in Barolo 89
- carbonnade 88
- chilli con carne 21
- Hungarian goulash 98
- massaman curry 116–17
- pot au feu 96–7
- rendang 113–15
- spicy Ethiopian stew 142–3
- stifado 90–2
- stroganoff, slow-cooked 93
- Vietnamese pho 118–20

beer and coriander, with Peruvian lamb stew 20

beetroot
- pecan, goat's cheese and puy lentil stew 50–1
- and Stilton, with beef 47

berbere spice mix 142–3

black bean stew, with chorizo and smoked pork 18

blanquette de veau 99–100

boeuf bourguignon 94

bouillabaisse 62–4

broad beans, sweetcorn and butternut squash, succotash of 26

broccoli and shitake mushrooms, with aromatic Thai chicken stew 110

browning meat 9

bulgur wheat 152

burnt pans 9

butternut squash, broad beans and sweetcorn, succotash of 26

C

cabbage
- ale and sausages, with pot roast pheasant 34–5
- *see also* red cabbage

caponata 102–3

cheese
- goat's, puy lentil, beetroot and pecan stew 50–1
- Swiss fondue 104

cherry tomatoes
- chicken cacciatore 72
- and coriander, with sweet potato dhal 124
- salt cod and chickpea stew 60–1

chestnuts, port and orange with venison 49

chicken 8
- aromatic Thai stew, with broccoli and shitake mushrooms 110
- Bahian stew 22–3
- cacciatore 72
- cooked with garlic, bay leaves and white wine 65
- coq au vin 66–7
- green curry 106–8
- and peanut Ghanian stew 132
- Persian stew, with sour cherries and walnuts 126–9
- and prawn jambalaya 14–17
- and seafood paella 68–71
- stew, with cider, tarragon and asparagus 30–1
- Tunisian stew, with harissa and caraway 130

chickpeas
- cherry tomato and salt cod stew 60–1
- harira 134–5

ACKNOWLEDGEMENTS

There are so many people who have helped and inspired me, in one way or another, in the creation of this book. It's been an amazing experience and without the love, support, knowledge, belief and friendship of so many wonderful people the journey would have been very different.

Mum, Dad, Suzanna – thanks for supporting me to do **stewed!** from day one. Dad, who would have thought that you singing Peter, Paul and Mary's 'Stewball was a race horse' when I was little could have had such an effect on me!

Thanks to Kathryn. Without you **stewed!** would not have been possible.
Thank you for believing in me.

Thank you Mark for holding the fort when I was up to my eyes in recipe development and trips to the shops.

Kathy, Paul and Theo – without your pots life would have been much harder over the last few months!

Penny, you've been a tireless recipe tester for me. Thank you. Also, Alastair, thank you for persevering with black beans. Sonya, Joher and Zelah – your chilli guidelines were a godsend.

Sarah L., thank you for believing in **stewed!** and taking on the cookbook project.

Helena, many thanks for your eagle-eyed copy editing.

Jonathan, Sunil, Tamin, Katy, Liz – an amazing team.
Thank you so much for creating such beautiful images.

Inga – you're a genius. How you keep coming up with the perfect designs for everything we do at **stewed!** astounds me.

Sarah K. – our cheese and wine extravaganza in Leadenhall Market seems a long time ago but, for me, it was the beginning of the journey. Thank you for spurring me on.

Rudi – cheers for the salt cod …

Alice, Mauro, Steve, Cee, Bernie, Peter, Simon, Sarah K. and Oli – thanks for being the best stew party guests a stew maker could hope to have.
Special thanks to Oli for squashing Boston baked beans into my carpet.

stewed!

NOURISH
YOUR
SOUL